The
Friends of the Library
have donated this book
to honor
Virginia Emerson
Friend of the Year
2004

City Birding

City Birding

True Tales of Birds and Birdwatching in Unexpected Places

Kenn Kaufman

Marie Winn

Paul A. Johnsgard

John Nichols

Mark S. Garland

Julie Zickefoose

Curtis Badger

James Gorman

Mary Durant

Clay Sutton

Ann Zwinger

Kim Todd

Judith A. Toups

Paul Kerlinger

Lawrence Kilham

Nikki Weinstein

Michael Harwood

STACKPOLE BOOKS

Published by
STACKPOLE BOOKS
5067 Ritter Road
Mechanicsburg, PA 17055
www.stackpolebooks.com

Printed in the United States of America

10 9 8 7 6 5 4 3 2 1

First edition

Edited by Mark Allison

For information on permissions and copyrights of individual stories,
see page 181.

Library of Congress Cataloging-in-Publication Data

City birding : true tales of birds and birdwatching in unexpected places
/ Kenn Kaufman ... [et al.].— 1st ed.
    p. cm.
  ISBN 0-8117-0027-5
  1. Bird watching—Anecdotes. 2. Birds—Anecdotes. 3. Urban
animals—Anecdotes. I. Kaufman, Kenn.
  QL677.5 .C548 2003
  598'.07'234—dc21   2002009268

Contents

Editor's note: Many birding and scientific publications capitalize the complete names of bird species; many publications aimed at a more general audience do not. The decision of whether or not to capitalize the species names in each of these stories was left to the story's author.

City Birding

Brooklyn's Rare Bird

An unlikely visitor causes a commotion
on Avenue X

Marie Winn

L ate one fall in a marsh in Lapland, or perhaps it was
on the banks of the Yenisey River in central Siberia—
far, far away, in any event—a bunch of large shorebirds
began to gather in flocks and wait for the right weather.
A good strong wind from the northwest was what they
needed to help them reach their distant wintering
grounds in Southern China, Thailand, or Vietnam.

One day when conditions seemed perfect they took
off. But along the way a freak storm caught the flock in
its path, blowing the birds completely off course. One
confused young male wandered miles in the wrong direction, clear across the Bering Strait and into Alaska.

For a few days the stray bird rested and fed in the
company of local shorebirds. Many belonged to his own
family, sandpipers, and a few to his very genus, *Tringa*,
but none were exactly like him. For one thing, his new

companions were genetically programmed to head directly south at this season, while his own species' inherited tendency was to go southeast, which is just what he did, making his way across an entire continent until he came to a coast.

That, quite possibly, is how a spotted redshank, *Tringa erythropus*, one of the rarest of all rare bird visitors to North America, happened to end up in a dingy little neighborhood marina in Brooklyn, New York.

On December 6 of that same year, John Yrizarry and his wife Mary, long-time Brooklyn residents, decided to make a little detour on their way home from shopping. The Brooklyn Christmas Bird Count was just a few weeks away, and Mr. Yrizarry, a renowned bird artist, was in charge of one counting area. He wanted to check out a small marina near Sheepshead Bay just at the intersection of Knapp Street and Avenue X. It was an unlikely spot, but last year he had seen some greater yellowlegs there. These large sandpipers are common shorebirds in the area, but they're not always around for the Christmas count.

A Christmas count, as you may know, is an annual bird census that takes place throughout the country during the final weeks of December. It was started in 1900 as an alternative to the traditional Christmas "side hunt," a gruesome competition during which hunters went out after

Marie Winn

Christmas dinner, chose sides, and tried to shoot as many birds as they could. Today volunteer bird-lovers get together around Christmas to count the different species of birds in an area as well as the numbers of individuals. This provides useful scientific data about bird populations. But Christmas counts are still competitive. Brooklyn really wants to beat Montauk, at the other end of Long Island, in total number of species. And teams in every area dream of finding a rare bird.

At the marina, Mr. Yrizarry immediately sighted some greater yellowlegs roosting on a broken-down wooden float in the murky water. The birds were asleep. He focused his binoculars on them for a moment. Then he rushed back to the car where his wife, a birdwatcher as well, was waiting patiently with the groceries.

"Mary! Get out! Five yellowlegs and one of them has red-orange legs!" he exclaimed. If this bird was what he thought it was, then it fell into the category described by Kenn Kaufman in his *Field Guide to Advanced Birding* as "a cosmic mind-bender."

Using a telescope he keeps in the trunk of his car for just such contingencies, Mr. Yrizarry now noted other signs suggesting that the bird, though closely resembling a yellowlegs, was in fact an excitingly different creature. There was less streaking on the crown, for one thing, and a longer eyeline.

Just then the mystery bird raised its head. Mr. Yrizarry quickly inspected its bill before the bird tucked it away again and resumed sleeping. Yes, a droop to the tip as if it had been hit by a hammer. And yes, bright red-orange on half the lower mandible. That was the clincher. Only one bird has all those features, and Mr. Yrizarry had last seen it in 1974 on his honeymoon with Mary. But that was in Europe where the bird is a regular visitor. Here was another one just a short drive from home. Mr. Yrizarry turned to his wife and said: "Do you know, I believe we have a spotted redshank here."

Within minutes of his discovery Mr. Yrizarry reported the bird to the Rare Bird Alert, a telephone hot line for unusual bird sightings. Birders from far and wide soon made their way to see the amazing visitor. Then two days later the bird vanished.

On December 18, the day before the Christmas count, the spotted redshank reappeared at the Knapp Street marina. There it was spotted in turn by Starr Saphir, one of the city's best birders and the captain of one of the thirteen teams of the Brooklyn count. Just before notifying the Rare Bird Alert that the redshank was back, she called Dorothy Poole, a friend who would be on her team the next day. When you think that some birders go all the way to Madagascar to acquire a new bird for their life list, it is not surprising that Ms. Poole dropped everything at the Manhattan office where she works as a market researcher and flagged a taxi to take her to the southeast corner of Brooklyn.

Word of the redshank's return spread rapidly. Even before sunrise on December 19, the day of the count, three birders had already set up telescopes at the marina. Six greater yellowlegs were there too, sleeping on the float. But no spotted redshank.

By three that afternoon a sizable crowd of disappointed redshank seekers were gathered at the marina. Rick Cech, a vice president at J. P. Morgan & Co. and a notable birder, was among them. He was the organizer of the Brooklyn count and he badly wanted a redshank on Brooklyn's list. That would settle Montauk's hash. At almost four-thirty, just as everyone was about to call it a day, a young man from Starr Saphir's team appeared with a breathless message: "We have it!"

I was a member of that team. We had counted thousands of common birds all day, ring-billed and herring gulls, mallards and brant, first at Rockaway Inlet and then at the huge Marine Park golf course. At a few minutes after four we reached a little saltwater pond just east of a semi-wild promontory called Plumb Beach. It was our last stop on the count—the sun would be setting within the next half hour.

As we approached we could see three birds feeding in the mud at the water's edge. Without much hope we peered at them through binoculars. And almost at the same moment we realized that the smallest of those three birds was the redshank. It had bright red-orange legs. It scuttled about a bit more nervously than the other two. We watched it for another moment or two, just to be sure. An odd, slightly creepy yet exhilarated feeling came over us and we hugged each other. Then our youngest teammate, a graduate student named David Krauss, raced to his car to get word to the crowd at the Knapp Street marina.

The light was rapidly fading by the time the others arrived. They could barely make out the color of the bird's legs, but they could easily see the differences in size and behavior. There was no doubt in anyone's mind that our bird was the spotted redshank.

One of those late arrivals introduced herself to me in the lowering light: Anna Kozlenko, a visiting ornithologist from the Moscow Research Institute of Natural History and Conservation. She had seen a spotted redshank only once before in her life. It was late last May, she told me, on the banks of the Yenisey River in central Siberia. I felt a chill. We exchanged a look and I knew we were both thinking the same astonishing thought.

Montauk chalked up 130 species on their Christmas count that year. Brooklyn had only 128. But one of them was a spotted redshank.

•

Marie Winn is the author of the best-selling *Red-Tails in Love* and has written about birding in New York City for *The Wall Street Journal* and *The New York Times*. She lives in Manhattan.

Urban Blight Birding

Birds boldly go where people
fear to tread

Paul Kerlinger

For more than a dozen years I have been exploring the waterways and islands that comprise the New York–New Jersey Harbor in order to study the birds that live there. Most of this area is seldom birded. In fact, it is inhospitable, dirty, and mostly inaccessible. When Rich Kane, vice president for conservation of the New Jersey Audubon Society, first told me that he and I were going to team up to study bird habitat along the Arthur Kill, the heavily industrialized waterway that separates New Jersey and Staten Island, I thought he was insane. I immediately dismissed the idea, secretly calling it the "Last Shreds" project. (There couldn't be more than a few insignificant shreds of habitat in this area, I believed.)

But he persisted, and my introductory tutorial on urban blight birds turned out to be a day to remember. Along the concrete-lined, trash-strewn tributaries of the Arthur Kill and the adjoining Raritan Bay, Rich and I, along with writer and naturalist Rick Radis, found some of the highest densities and largest diversities of migrating songbirds I'd seen anywhere. In one small stand of pin oaks, some of which may have been a hundred years old, we managed to identify twenty-three species of warblers as tractor trailers rumbled nearby. And we discovered remnant forests and salt marshes that had somehow escaped the onslaught of local factory and highway construction and the creation of nearby tank farms and refineries. I was humbled by my partners' birding skills (and their knowledge of local delicatessens). They knew how good such urban settings could be for birding, and they were sharing their secret with me.

During another morning of urban blight birding Rich and I found perhaps a hundred thrushes in a mature stand of oaks in a city park after a thunderstorm grounded them just before dawn. We saw Swainson's Thrushes, Wood Thrushes, and Veery. When these migrants landed, they undoubtedly saw only the forest canopy. There was no understory—under the trees were only grass and bare earth. The birds were feeding in the open and easy to watch. From the edge of the park we could see traffic on the New Jersey Turnpike.

One of my most unforgettable birding experiences along the Arthur Kill was standing on top of a car parked in a cemetery to peer over a tall fence and observe cormorants and Pied-billed Grebes feeding in a pond near the Bayway refinery in Elizabeth—the same facility that was responsible for spilling more than a hundred thousand gallons of oil into the Arthur Kill in 1990. (Since then, the facility was sold to Tosco, whose double-hulled tankers and greater vigilance have resulted in cleaner water; Tosco, in fact, has become a cooperator in the New York City Audubon Society's research efforts.) The fact that grebes and cormorants were actively feeding on fish within a few hundred feet of one of the world's largest tank farms helped erase my lingering doubts about urban blight birding.

During my initial visits to the Arthur Kill and its tributaries, I often wondered what was on the islands on the Staten Island side of the river. Here, Pralls Island was visible, as was Isle of Meadows in the shadow of the Fresh Kills landfill—New York City's mountain of garbage. Both were forested and didn't look to be part of their urban setting. And I remembered that once while crossing the Verrazano Narrows Bridge from Brooklyn to Staten Island I saw two other small islands, Hoffman and Swinburne, about a mile off the south shore of Staten Island. I realized that in the midst of some of the highest-priced real estate in the world were at least four uninhabited islands.

During a survey of a small impoundment along the Rahway River, a tributary of the Arthur Kill, I finally learned what was on some of those islands. Upon arriving, Rich and I immediately saw two Snowy Egrets and one Great Egret feeding in the shallows. There were also three Double-crested Cormorants fishing in the lake and a Common Yellowthroat and several other migrant warblers in the thick brush along the water's edge. We also turned up a few Short-billed Dowitchers and a Spotted Sandpiper feeding a short distance from the egrets. I was stunned when Rich told me that hundreds of egrets, herons, and ibis, along with Herring and Great Black-backed gulls, nested on Pralls Island and Isle of Meadows and also on Shooters Island farther north, and that the birds we were watching had probably flown ten or fifteen miles to feed in the waters in front of us. I suddenly realized just how important these seemingly filthy little urban waterways really are.

As fate would have it, about five years after my experiences along the Arthur Kill and Raritan Bay, I was asked by New York City Audubon to survey fall migrants at Bayswater Point State Park and Dubos Sanctuary in the Rockaway section of Queens. Again, I was dubious at first, even though I knew how great the birding was in the Jamaica Bay Refuge. Within a few days, however, I found some really good birds at Bayswater and Dubos, including American Bittern; Red-shouldered Hawk; American

Woodcock; and Seaside, Sharp-tailed, and Vesper sparrows. There were also good numbers of more common migrants: warblers, thrushes, gnatcatchers, and other sparrows by the hundreds.

There were two distinct drawbacks to birding these sites, though. Dubos Sanctuary is directly across Jamaica Bay from JFK, and the first time I heard the Concorde take off on its ten A.M. flight to Paris I hit the deck. It took me more than a few seconds to regain my composure. The other drawback was personal safety. I discovered it was best to do my surveys early, before the bad guys came out, and when I was done it was always a thrill to see my car parked where I left it, windows intact. (That the area was not an especially nice place was evident from a pit bull skull I once found there. It had a bullet hole in it.) I personally never had a problem at Bayswater or Dubos, however.

A year later, New York City Audubon asked me to manage the Harbor Herons Project, continuing their long-term heron and egret population monitoring study on the harbor islands—including the islands I'd seen from the Jersey side of the Arthur Kill. The society had begun the project in the early '80s when it learned that herons and egrets had recolonized some islands in the Arthur Kill and the East River after decades of absence. It's a long-term population study that focuses on evaluating the status of the islands' heron populations and the protection of nesting habitat. During my very first visits to the islands, and after discussions with Dr. Kathy Parsons of the Manomet Observatory, who had conducted the Harbor Herons surveys for ten years, I learned a lot. Most importantly, I discovered that the New York–New Jersey Harbor islands were rich with bird life and really worth preserving.

Five years after taking over the project, I had expanded the study from five islands to about fourteen. I also began to study other bird species. With the help of a group of dedicated volunteers, I monitored the nesting populations of Black- and Yellow-crowned night-herons; Great, Snowy, and Cattle egrets; Little Blue Herons; Glossy Ibis; and even a few Tricolored and Green herons. On each island, my team and I counted the active nests, eggs, and young of all these species. The Harbor Herons study provided me with some of my most vivid urban birding memories.

In particular, exploring North and South Brother islands, at the confluence of the East River, the Harlem River, and the Long Island Sound, offered some unforgettable experiences. Getting to the islands required a boat ride through what is called Hell Gate, a narrowing of the East River where the water is shallow and the currents are often overpowering. I ran through Hell Gate several times in a nineteen-foot outboard: a harrowing commute. (I never understood how nonplussed Kathy seemed to be when she piloted the boat.) I eventually used what I thought would be a safer means of transport to the islands, but on my first trip to North Brother aboard a New York City Department of Environmental Protection vessel, the captain hit a submerged pier, bending the propeller shaft. We limped back to Randalls Island, but I got my data.

At one time, North Brother Island was the location of the sanitorium in which the infamous Typhoid Mary was institutionalized and where she eventually died. Today, only the decaying ruins of the sanitorium's brick buildings, docks, and houses remain. I'll never forget walking by old gas-lamp-posts, stepping over crumbling curbstones, and pushing through tangles of poison ivy, bittersweet, and senescent apple trees as I moved among Black-crowned Night-Heron nests on North Brother.

Farther north and east, in the Bronx, is Goose Island, a one-acre part of Pelham Bay Park that exists literally in the shadow of Co-op City, a twenty-plus-story cooperative complex in which thousands of people live. The island is also within a hundred yards of the Metro North Commuter Train line and about a hundred and fifty yards from the Hutchinson River Parkway and the New England Thruway. Despite constant loud and obtrusive disturbances, about 100 pairs of Black- and Yellow-crowned night-herons, Great and Snowy egrets, and Little Blue Herons nest on Goose Island. Go figure.

Isle of Meadows in the Arthur Kill may be my favorite island of all those in the study. The island is so close to the now-closed Fresh Kills landfill that I used to be able to hear the voices of workers on the off-loading docks as they moved the city's garbage from barges to trucks. The beeping of the cranes was continual, and the pungent aroma from empty barges drifted over the forested heronry whenever the wind came from the south. But on this thoroughly industrialized landscape were more than seven hundred pairs of nesting herons and egrets, along with hundreds of other non-nesting species, including Barn Owls, Cooper's Hawks, Northern Harriers, Baltimore Orioles, and more than a dozen species of migrating warblers, including Connecticut Warblers. Along the salt marsh at the edge of the island were Marsh Wren and Willow Flycatcher nests.

Colonial nesting birds are not the only avian life on the islands in the New York–New Jersey Harbor. On tiny Huckleberry Island in Long Island Sound, just outside the Bronx, American Oystercatchers nest. Willets nest along the salt marsh of Canarsie Pol in Jamaica Bay, and in winter, Brant surround some of the bay's islands. Various songbirds and raptors, including Gray Catbirds, Willow

Flycatchers, Eastern Towhees, Song Sparrows, Marsh Wrens, and Barn Owls, nest on the region's islands. On Shooters Island, in the shadow of the Bayonne Bridge between Staten Island and Jersey City, a single-day survey of nearly four hundred heron nests also revealed about fifteen species of migrant warblers, birds that were heading north to boreal spruce-fir and deciduous forests that decided to stop and rest in the island's thickets of Japanese honeysuckle and gray birch.

In 2001, two Ospreys built a nest on a derelict piling on Shooters Island, seemingly oblivious to tugboats and tanker ships passing only a hundred yards away, not to mention the bumper-to-bumper traffic on the Bayonne Bridge and the 737s landing at nearby Newark International. This pair was probably the first Osprey nesting record in modern times in the Arthur Kill. Two other Osprey nests were known to be farther downstream, one on a smokestack of an abandoned building and the other perhaps on an exposed part of a sunken tugboat or barge that is part of a rusting steel boneyard there. These nests are quite safe: predators would be risking their lives trying to get close to them.

In the years that I have conducted the Harbor Herons program I've introduced hundreds of people to these islands and their avian inhabitants. Almost every person is stunned that the islands are so rich in bird life yet so damned filthy. My wife once asked me why we didn't clean up the tires, lumber, bottles, cans, and other sundry flotsam and jetsam that cover the islands. I described how gulls literally nest in the trash and how we found nests in old tires and sections of rotting docks that had floated up over the years. Besides, once the existing junk was removed, more trash would only bob back up on the next tide. And it's more than likely that the littered shorelines and wrecked vessels, docks, and barges keep people away.

By becoming the birder-scientist who monitored colonial waterbirds in the New York–New Jersey Harbor, I had come full circle. In 1972, I was not an avid birder. I knew feeder birds, most hawks, and a few warblers, but almost never went into the field with the sole intent of looking at birds. That changed during an evening fishing trip at Playland in Rye, north of New York City. While fishing a rocky islet about a quarter mile offshore, an interesting bird landed nearby. The bird intrigued me, partly because it and I both seemed to be fishing. I asked a fellow angler what it was, and he told me it was a Black-crowned Night-Heron. I watched the bird fishing at the edge of the rippling water, with the Manhattan skyline in the background and the sun setting behind it. I was entranced. I remember catching some striped bass that evening, but I realize now it was that night-heron that had me hooked.

•

Paul Kerlinger is a former director of the Cape May Bird Observatory, coauthor of *The New York City Audubon Society Guide to Finding Birds in the Metropolitan Area*, and author of *How Birds Migrate*. He lives on Cape May Point.

Central Park Irregular

Binoculars and a field guide
do not a birder make

Nikki Weinstein

I was sixteen years old, a sophomore in high school, and halfway through a semester of Wildlife Ecology at my tiny New Hampshire high school when I first encountered birding. We had just completed a two-week section on birds of the White Mountains and were out in the field for a pop quiz. My grade rode on just one question. "Ms. Weinstein," my teacher called out. "What is that?" He pointed skyward—the general direction of a shrill *tweet-tweet-tweet*. We had devoted an entire class period to distinguishing the recordings of various bird songs; I had taken copious notes and finished all the outside reading. Cocking my head to convey deep thought, I looked at my teacher and gave my answer. "I would have to say that's a bird, sir."

The fact is I've always ignored the details in favor of a vague "would you look at that mountain!" approach to the natural world. But after six years of living in

Manhattan, the manic pace of the city had begun to seep into the very fiber of my being. Like so many others who have moved from greener locales to carve out a home on this island of skyscraper mountains and paved-street pastures, I ached for the Great Outdoors. Still, I am a New Yorker, and I began to believe that in order to find a true Arcadia, Gortex must be purchased and a bridge or tunnel must be crossed. So I was thrilled when a colleague recently told me about the Central Park Christmas Bird Count, a competitive event undertaken by the city's die-hard birders and with the purpose of doing exactly what its name professes. In the middle of New York, urban sprawl had come to a screeching stop, and it seemed that only this quiet, informal group of binocular-toting folks knew it; they managed to pierce the park's tame exterior of fountains and playgrounds to reveal a bit of nature as untamed as that in Westchester County, or even Connecticut. The annual count had passed me by, but there was much more than just that going on, my colleague assured me; from the way she told it, every day in the park was a true-life special on Animal Planet. I was determined to get in on the action.

A Google search under "New York + Birding" revealed more than three thousand hits—a whopping number that disabused me of the notion that I would be joining a secret society of naturalists. In fact, birding is a thriving Manhattan hobby, and although it is largely unknown to those who do not participate, it is widespread. Among the many Internet hits, I found a site called Virtualbirder.com that provides a Rare Bird Alert posting—my first clue that birders are a breed known for data collection: the trophies of their hunts are the recognition and notation of a various species.

In order to take part in this activity, I needed to learn a few facts, and so I began to study, first examining *The New York City Audubon Society Guide to Finding Birds in the Metropolitan Area*, edited by Paul Kerlinger and Marcia T. Fowle (a woman whose purpose in life was enviably predetermined by her name). The guide proved to be loaded with information such as the migratory routes that make Central Park a five-star stopover for hundreds of species of birds each spring and fall, turning the place into an excellent birding site. The *Peterson Field Guide to Eastern Birds* provided me with ample illustrations to memorize and fodder for fantasies of seeing a saw-whet owl or hearing a loon. I picked up an issue of *Birder's World* magazine, added Birding.com to my list of bookmarks for its suggestions on New York excursions as near as Jamaica Bay Wildlife Refuge and as far as Niagara Falls. And slowly, book by book, site by site, I began to fall in love with my new hobby; the fact that I had yet to set foot in the park or even buy a pair of binoculars seemed wholly irrelevant.

When I read Marie Winn's *Red-Tails in Love*, an account of hawks that improbably chose a Fifth Avenue apartment building for their nest site (as well as providing Ms. Winn a 317-page opportunity to display superior birding skills of which I was already jealous), I savored every paragraph. Winn turned Central Park birding into a series of expeditions as feral as Charles Camsell's 1914 Arctic Land Expedition, and by the time I finished the book I knew that those who plunge into the park's depths, encountering baby raccoons, spotting nesting orioles, picking wild mushrooms, and learning the elusive answer to Holden Caulfield's probing question about where the ducks go when the ponds freeze over, live lives far richer than the rest of us who pass by the park oblivious to the wilds within. My imagination ignited at once; perhaps my research would enable me to become one of Winn's "regulars," roaming the Ramble in a woolen hat, an insulated mug of herbal tea in my hand, marveling at the first phoebes to make it back after winter. That this event would require an entire personality transformation did not occur to me.

At last the day arrived for my first outing, a crack-of-dawn guided tour led by the New York City Audubon Society. I had bought myself a pair of Smith & Wesson binoculars just the day before. I headed into the park. In order to insure some time with the Central Park Bird Register, I arrived a half-hour early at the Boat House, where the nearly mythic book—an informal binder democratically available to anyone who wants to add field notes and observations—can always be found. The setting was ideal—winter's first snow began to fall early that morning—and I sat by the fire in a room empty but for a few tenacious early-morning explorers. Opening the book at random, I read my first entry:

> Screech Owl found dead on 79th Street Transverse sidewalk on 1/1; pink nail polish on face; transmitter still attached; no obvious sign of injury; no blood, but possible broken wing.

Not exactly the tenderly written paean to owl love I would have preferred. And frankly, I couldn't remember a single thing about screech-owls, or if I had read anything about them at all. Suddenly, all my research became a blur, and I realized that the only birds I was able to recognize were those standing still on the pages of the *Peterson Field Guide*. Doubt began to corrode my enthusiasm. Why, I wondered, did the entry's author bother to note the color of the nail polish on the dead bird's face? Did it matter one lick if it was Parisian Pink or Cotton Candy? But science-minded folks note *everything*—how had I forgotten that? Suddenly, years of science classes came flooding back, and I remembered who I was: the girl that only recalled the difference between a stalagmite and a stalactite because "stalactites hang tight." Had my best friend not creatively turned the Periodic Table of Elements into a hip-hop song (Na just happens to rhyme with "boot-tay"), I might have done enough damage to my GPA to miss out on college altogether. Birding is a scientific activity, and although it's usually practiced by amateurs, it's not likely to replace bungee jumping anytime soon. What had I been thinking?

I joined the group gathering outside—a gaggle of mostly elderly ladies with high-powered binoculars hanging around their necks that made my cheap pair look positively impotent. "Do you know how to focus them?" one woman asked, giving my Smith & Wessons a pitying glance. I didn't. Just as I succeeded in following her kindly instructions by focusing on a distant garbage can, Audrey, the guide, announced that a starling had landed on the top of a nearby bush. Whirling around with the binoculars still held up to my face, I induced a rush of motion sickness so nauseating that I dropped the binoculars and shut my eyes, not caring that I had missed the bird. "Are you okay?" asked Audrey, as she handed me the banged-up binoculars from the ground. I draped the strap around my neck for safety's sake and nodded mutely.

While I regained my composure, Audrey explained that the starling is a highly adaptable bird, introduced to our tender ecosystem by a lover of literature who fancied the idea of bringing every bird ever mentioned by Shakespeare to the United States. After everyone in our small group (but me) caught sight of it, we moved up the footpath into the depths of the Ramble and toward the Point, an area Winn fondly mentions for its prime birding. Gazing into a wall of naked branches, someone spotted a white-throated sparrow, vaguely offering "the upper branch of that tree over there" as the target spot. I lifted my binoculars in the general direction of a brown flutter to discover that I had absolutely no idea what I was looking at.

Interestingly, for all my research, I had not encountered a single how-to on binocular use, but I believe it's needed. Looking into a patch of bare trees bereft of distinction, I would select my point of focus, lift the binoculars to my eyes, and lose all points of reference. Had anyone been watching our group they would have noticed a throng of people gathered together, all pointing their binoculars skyward in silent rapture while I stood a pace apart, directing the binoculars at the toes of my boots and dragging them slowly toward my destination—in this case forked branches where a sparrow had been just a moment before. "Did you see it?" Audrey asked me, a note of concern in her voice when she caught me using my binoculars to stare at an old Snickers wrapper on the ground. "It's beautiful," I lied.

"A cardinal!" someone whispered. The flash of crimson streaked across the dull, gray patch of woods and the garish little guy hopped onto the ground less than ten yards from us. I adore this bird because it's red and easy to spot—a fat bandit in an ebony mask stealing tiny specks from the ground. The food was leftover bounty scattered from the feeders—pregnant sacks of seed hanging from the trees and generously restocked by park regulars. For me, this site provided much more than a touching gesture of goodwill toward the birds; it was an opportunity to actually get a few different species in my cross hairs and study what had, until this day, been merely academic.

I stood quietly by the feeders, watching hearty New York birds feast like invulnerable Romans. At last I had found my own live nature special, even if it was one that reeked of human intervention. For the sake of birders who crave a good peek at the objects of their passion, Darwinism has been ignored; the piles of feed attract hordes of species, all beleaguered by the scarcity of winter. It was a thrill to test my skills of recognition without the need for binoculars—and in fact, I wasn't so bad. I saw a tufted titmouse steal a beak-full of seeds and fly it over to a cement block in which it stashed its bounty. I watched a starling bully past a fox sparrow, pushing the poor creature to another sack of seed. Just as I allowed myself to feel confident, however, a well-intentioned woman redirected our attention to the trees. "Look! A yellow-bellied sapsucker!" The animal was hanging off the trunk of a distant tree—I experienced technical difficulties and never saw it, but I immediately took to the sapsucker for enduring a name as cruel as a playground taunt.

As I stood gazing into middle space through my binoculars, looking for something with a yellow belly or sucking sap, a throaty voice cut through the chorus of *oohs* that were emitted in succession as one by one the group caught sight of the woodpecker. "There's a lovely pair of Coopers a small ways up the path," said the voice. The women all lowered their binoculars and tottered in the direction given. As I followed, I snuck a glance at the man who had informed us of the birds: an English bloke in his twenties with dyed-black hair reaching past his shoulders and dressed in a black leather jacket, well-worn jeans, and biker boots. Had it not been for the telltale binoculars hanging from his neck, I might have expected him to be enjoying a breakfast Bud at an East Village bar.

Some might marvel at the local birding for the migratory routes and the sheer surprise of finding so much wildlife in the middle of a steel-and-cement landscape. I was smitten with the birders themselves. In a city known for its diversity, even this humble pursuit manages to bring together a retired high school art teacher from New Jersey, an Upper East Side matron, and a downtown devotee of punk. But I could only look for a moment—the Coopers beckoned.

As the tour wore on, my success with the binoculars improved, and I even managed to catch sight of a distant, half-hidden wood duck. But the truth is, I was able to enjoy the oddly capped, beautifully colored animal even more when I went home and examined the illustration on page fifty-one of the *Peterson Field Guide*.

My first birding tour proved to be an ideal way to enjoy the first snowfall of the season, but for me the birds came second to simply being outside. Before heading back to the subway that afternoon, I stopped by the Boat House to spend a little more time with the Register. This time, my anxiety had mellowed and I was able to enjoy what I read.

January 2, 2002

One notable bird today: a female Cowbird to go with the male spotted yesterday. It was at the Central Park Zoo with 20-plus Common Grackles.

Had I read anything about cowbirds? I really couldn't remember. All at once I realized that while I might have been meant to be a birdwatcher, I would never be a regular. I just couldn't muster up the excitement that my compatriots seemed to have for the birds. While they marveled at the wingspan of a soaring red-tail, I was much more content to stand in the Ramble and catch snowflakes on my tongue. But even though I proved to be a rather inept birder, I'm not ready to give up the habit altogether. I'll probably be in the park this spring when migratory season rolls around, and when I tire of the birds—as I inevitably will—I'll be the one with a pair of binoculars dangling around my neck, looking for wildflowers.

•

Nikki Weinstein is a writer who lives in Manhattan, where she watches birds, occasionally.

Birding on the Bridge

Big rigs, concrete, and miles of open sea

Curtis Badger

A tractor trailer rumbled by, gaining speed as it exited the tunnel, but the flock of sea ducks paid it no mind. The scoters and oldsquaws were diving for mussels, and the trucks and cars zipping by a few hundred feet away were of no consequence.

We were on the Chesapeake Bay Bridge-Tunnel, a seventeen-mile span that connects Hampton Roads with Virginia's Eastern Shore at the mouth of the Chesapeake Bay. The bridge-tunnel has become one of the hottest birding spots in the east, even though it has none of the landscape features we normally associate with good birding. There are no grasslands, no shrubby undergrowth, no swamps and marshes, and there's not a tree for miles around.

What we have here is concrete and water, an unlikely combination to provide a day of exceptional birdwatching. Oh yes, we do have our eighteen-wheelers, huge, lumbering giants hauling everything from cornflakes to car parts up and down the east coast. And there are SUVs hauling vacationing families, businesspeople in Chevy sedans, and college kids in their Hondas.

My wife Lynn and I were on the bridge-tunnel one recent winter morning, and we noticed that once you get down to the business of scoping out birds, you forget about the traffic, just as the sea ducks do. The bridge-tunnel has four man-made islands, each anchoring the opening of a tunnel, and the paved areas atop these islands are where you go to watch birds. So the trucks go by, disappear into a tunnel, and are gone until they reach the other end. You're near the traffic, but never in harm's way.

When the Chesapeake Bay Bridge-Tunnel was built in the early 1960s, it was considered a wonder of modern engineering, a tribute to the ability of humans to conquer a formidable natural landscape. Here we had seventeen miles of open water, water that could often be nasty, the meeting place of the Atlantic Ocean and the Chesapeake Bay. The plan was to build a two-lane concrete bridge across this span, and, in order to accommodate the large ships that called in Hampton Roads and Baltimore, to also build two tunnels deep beneath the bottom. There were many who said it couldn't be done, but the engineers and construction crews proved them wrong. The bridge-tunnel opened to great fanfare in 1964, making obsolete the car ferries that once transported vehicles and passengers across the Virginia capes.

Not long after the bridge–tunnel was built, local fishermen made a surprising discovery. The span was a perfect fish magnet, the mother of all artificial reefs. The two tunnels are anchored by huge rock piles built upon the bay bottom, one at the end of each tunnel. These rocks attract shellfish such as mussels and oysters, and the crevices between them are great hiding places for crabs, small fish, shrimp, and other crustaceans. Larger fish such as gray trout, flounder, and striped bass take note of this, and these predators come to the rock islands on a regular basis in search of a free meal. Two–legged predators do likewise, making the bridge–tunnel one of the most popular saltwater fishing destinations on the east coast.

Birders didn't catch on quite so quickly as the fishermen, but during the 1980s and early '90s, an increasing number of people began to realize that the shellfish and baitfish living among the rocks attracted predators other than the finned variety. In winter, huge rafts of sea ducks would gather around the rock islands, diving for their dinner. If you were willing to bundle up and get out there on the islands with your binoculars and scope, you could see some pretty amazing birds.

When the bridge-tunnel first opened, only one of the islands was open to the public, the southernmost island you cross soon after paying the toll at the Virginia Beach plaza. This island is home to the Sea Gull Restaurant and Gift Shop and a fishing pier. A scenic walkway was built atop the tunnel entrance, complete with industrial-strength binoculars on metal posts anchored to the sidewalk like artillery pieces. The idea was to have travelers stop at the restaurant for a bite to eat and then enjoy the walkway, using the binoculars to watch the Navy ships and tankers coming and going a short distance away.

Well, by golly, someone was checking out an aircraft carrier one February day when those binoculars focused instead on the waters below. There were birds down there—a lot of them. Word spread through the birding community that the bridge-tunnel was the place to go in winter to get a close-up look at sea ducks, eiders, and gannets. And after a storm, a great many unusual species could be seen.

Lynn and I live about a one-hour drive north of the bridge-tunnel and try to get down there two or three times over the winter. Just ahead of an approaching storm is usually a good time to go, for the quality birding if not the creature comforts. We use the bridge-tunnel frequently when traveling, but a few times a year we simply pay the ten-dollar toll and spend the day on the rock islands of the bridge. When we last visited, I showed my permit to the toll booth attendant (the bridge-tunnel has opened all four islands to birding, providing that birders get an annual letter of permission and present it to the toll taker when entering the bridge), and he picked up his two-way radio and announced, "birdwatchers in a green pickup," thus alerting bridge-tunnel police that we would be stopping on the islands.

"Do you get many of us?" I asked.

He laughed. "You'll have some company out there today."

It was late January, and as soon as we reached open water we saw scoters, great rafts of them bobbing along on the waves and trading back and forth along the horizon. Vehicles are not allowed to stop on the bridge itself, and at fifty-five miles an hour the scoters were black dots. "What kind of scoters are those?" I asked Lynn.

"At fifty-five, they're all black scoters," she said.

But within a few minutes we were on the first island and we quickly picked out the surf scoters, with their colorful bills and white napes, and the white-winged scoters, with the white commas under their eyes and the white chevrons on their secondary feathers. There were hundreds of them, perhaps thousands.

Two cars were parked at the end of the island where the tunnel tube disappears beneath the bay. Cormorants were perched on the rock jetty and a half-dozen people were scoping them out. There were great and double-crested cormorants, distinguishable by their size and by the dark-over-light breast color of the first-year great, compared to the light-over-dark configuration of the double-crested.

There also were countless oldsquaws, ruddy ducks, lesser scaup, redheads, and gulls, mainly ring-billed and herring. In the distance, on the ocean side of the island, we could see northern gannets soaring and diving. At the base of the islands the scoters were gathered, diving occasionally and bringing up black mollusks, possibly mussels. With the raft of scoters was a solitary common eider, a first-winter bird in its mottled brown and white plumage.

One of the other birders told us he had seen a harlequin duck farther south along the island, and we went in search of it, locating it after about five minutes. The harlequin was dozing along the outer perimeter of a raft of scoters, but I could pick up the cinnamon sides and white stripes outlining its breast. On the rocks below us ruddy turnstones foraged among the algae, and we saw a purple sandpiper in a pool created by a slight depression in a large rock.

We decided to drive on to the next island. Although the habitat is the same, it's a good idea to investigate all the islands because they sometimes hold surprises. The second island held what for us was a great prize, a handsome drake king eider. If the weather is sufficiently cold on the mainland, the bridge-tunnel can have some species not normally seen in open water. During a prolonged freeze a few winters ago, with the shallow bays and coves frozen over, black ducks and other surface-feeding ducks were regular visitors along the bridge-tunnel.

On the third island, a pair of snow buntings was in a grassy strip adjacent to the parking area. By the time we reached the fourth island we were ready for lunch, so we pulled over at the Sea Gull Restaurant and warmed up with sandwiches and clam chowder. The restaurant here is the only game in town unless you leave the bridge-tunnel or brown-bag your own, and the suspicion is that the menu is limited and overpriced. Not true. No gouging going on here. The food is good, the service is friendly and efficient, and the prices are fair. Indeed, the restaurant has the feel of a small-town diner, serving breakfast all day, lunch specials, and they even give you a coupon for free coffee and soft drinks when you pay the toll.

Unlike most small-town diners, however, the Sea Gull offers a commanding view. Lynn and I sat at the window and watched the ships sail past. On the water below us we could see red-breasted mergansers and oldsquaws bobbing on the swells. It's the only restaurant we've ever visited where we always bring along our binoculars and field guides.

The most appealing thing about birding the bridge-tunnel is the prospect of seeing a rare species. After Lynn and I finished lunch, we met a group from the College of William and Mary who had just spotted a Thayer's gull, a rare winter visitor in the east. Black-tailed gulls, natives of the Orient, have been seen along the span, attracting birders from around the country. The chances of observing rare seabirds are especially good after storms, when birds can be blown inland from their normal haunts far out to sea.

"The rule of thumb is that the worst the weather gets, the better the birding gets," says Patricia Sumners of the public relations office at the bridge-tunnel. "February is probably the best month because it's cold, windy, and stormy. If you want to see birds, that's the time to go. Just wrap up and get out there."

Sumners says that as word has spread of the bridge-tunnel as a birding venue, demand has increased for the annual permission letters, and requests are coming from all over the country. "We get about a thousand requests each year. People have come from Idaho, Minnesota, California. We even had a couple from the Netherlands who had heard about the black-tailed gull on a birding hot line and wanted to see it. Serious birders will travel a long distance and go to a lot of trouble to add a bird to their life list."

Interest in the bridge-tunnel as a birding destination is also helping the bottom line for the span, especially in mid-winter, when travel is usually at a low mark. "If you multiply each permission letter we issue by the ten-dollar fare, the economic impact is significant," says Sumners. "But most of the people visit several times, and they'll eat at the restaurant and spend some time either on the Eastern Shore or in Virginia Beach, so the total economic benefit to the community is difficult to measure, but it is very substantial."

Bridge-tunnel workers are also getting used to seeing people with binoculars and scopes during the worst winter weather. In the 1980s, the few birders who ventured out were indulged, sort of like the eccentric but harmless bachelor uncle. Now, birders are part of the winter landscape at the bridge-tunnel, almost a daily occurrence if the weather is sufficiently nasty.

When Lynn and I make a trip there, we usually include a few stops near the northern terminus of the complex. The bridge crosses Fisherman Island National Wildlife Refuge and skirts Eastern Shore of Virginia National Wildlife Refuge as it enters the Eastern Shore.

These two different refuges share the same administration and are separated only by Smith Island Inlet.

Fisherman Island has in recent years had large breeding populations of little blue herons, great egrets, black-crowned night-herons, brown pelicans, and various gulls and terns. A large colony of royal terns has been using the island, plus a few uncommon species such as white ibis and yellow-crowned night-herons. Although you pass through Fisherman Island when traveling on the bridge-tunnel, stopping is not allowed. The refuge does offer group tours on weekends through the winter, and a viewing area at the tip of the peninsula was constructed when the bridge was expanded to four lanes in 1998.

Birders are welcome, however, at the neighboring 650-acre mainland refuge, which until 1984 was a military installation. During World War II, gun emplacements were installed to protect the bay entrance; the Air Force operated a radar station at the site during the years following the war. At Eastern Shore, a short hiking trail covers woodland, open fields, and salt marsh. You can climb a set of steps and stand atop a gun emplacement and have a great view of Smith Island, Fisherman Island, the bridge-tunnel, and the expansive marshes. It's a fine spot for observing hawks during the fall migration, and plenty of warblers and resident birds can be seen in the thick understory. We like to visit in the spring and early summer and bring the scope. Several heronries are in the area, and the platform affords a great view of the marsh and surrounding waters. Songbirds can be seen along the trail and boardwalk, and the marshes usually yield tricolored herons, great blues, great and snowy egrets, rails, and various gulls and terns.

Three miles north of the refuge is Kiptopeke State Park on the Chesapeake Bay. Before the bridge-tunnel opened in 1964 Kiptopeke was the ferry terminal, and the breakwater of concrete ships still stands. The property changed hands several times during the post-ferry days, and finally the state bought it in 1991 and created a park, preserving some magnificent bluffs and maritime dune thickets.

Perhaps the best time to visit Kiptopeke is the fall, especially for warblers, vireos, thrushes, tanagers, and the like. The Virginia Society of Ornithology has operated a bird-banding station here since 1963, and visitors are welcome. The station usually opens during the first week of September and runs into November. During the migration, banders might see some one hundred different species. The most common is the yellow-rumped warbler, followed by the American redstart, common yellowthroat, black-throated blue warbler, and gray catbird. Other frequent catches include the hermit thrush, northern cardinal, rufous-sided towhee, blue jay, golden-crowned kinglet, American goldfinch, white-eyed vireo, and downy woodpecker. Usually there are a few surprises as well, such as Kentucky and Connecticut warblers, Louisiana water-thrush, American woodcock, and golden-winged warbler.

Kiptopeke is also a fine place to see hawks. An observation tower was constructed in the 1990s in a cooperative effort by the state park and the VSO. Frequent sightings include red-tailed, broad-winged, sharp-shinned, and Cooper's hawks. Bald eagles are on the comeback and are no longer rare sights. Northern harriers patrol the grassy fields east of the platform, and American kestrels are common from fall through spring. The concrete ships serve as a roosting area for rock dove, which are targets for peregrine falcons. Merlins can sometimes be seen hunting along the beach in fall and winter. A hawk-banding station operates near the platform.

The state park has constructed numerous trails and boardwalks, often taking advantage of roadways installed when developers planned to subdivide the property and sell lots during the '70s. The trails run through myrtle and cedar thickets and across a dune line to observation platforms overlooking the bay. The thickets are perfect places to see migrating birds during spring and fall, and the open water will provide winter sightings of buffle-heads, hooded and red-breasted mergansers, oldsquaws, and scoters. In winter, yellow-rumped warblers gather in the myrtle thickets by the thousands.

The remarkable thing about these birding areas is that they are within the radius of one of the busiest centers of commerce in the east. The mouth of the Chesapeake Bay sees a constant stream of military and commercial shipping. The Chesapeake Bay Bridge-Tunnel and U.S. Route 13 carry a high volume of traffic, and the highway literally bisects a wildlife refuge and brushes against a state park. Perhaps the lesson in this is that wild things are remarkably resilient and resourceful.

A bridge that attracts birds. Who would have thought it?

•

Curtis Badger has written widely about wildlife art and the history and natural history of the Virginia coast. His books include *Salt Tide* and *Bellevue Farm*. His most recent work is *Clams: How to Find, Catch, and Cook Them*. He lives on Virginia's Eastern Shore.

Duck Soup

Big, fat birds make easy targets
for the novice

James Gorman

I'm not the only one who likes to watch ducks in winter. David Allen Sibley does, too, although our interests
aren't exactly the same. I like ducks partly because I can't
identify little birds. They're too fast, they won't sit still, and
no matter how much I pore over the guidebooks, I always
conclude that I'm looking at a sparrow.

This is not Mr. Sibley's problem. He's the author of
The Sibley Guide to Birds, a vast, highly regarded and pre-
cisely detailed bird book. He doesn't have to look at ducks
just because they're big and they sit still; he can identify
anything he wants. Nonetheless he was more than toler-
ant when I called him to talk ducks.

"My wife and I do something that we call 'duck days'
in the winter," he said. A duck day involves getting in the
car and driving along a shoreline looking for bays where
ducks congregate. It's birding "from the comfort of the car

with a cup of coffee and your binoculars." To add to the pleasure, Sibley said, winter is the breeding season for many ducks, and the male birds are starting to display their brighter breeding colors. "From the duck's point of view, this is spring."

That's yet another reason to like ducks. They inspire optimism. A drake in breeding plumage bobbing happily in near-freezing water with mating on his mind makes you reconsider the nature of winter. This is the kind of feeling you don't get from hawks, for instance, which have always seemed rather chilly to me. Ducks also inspire laughter, as in the cases of Donald and Daffy. And they're cooperative. You can find them almost anywhere there's water, and with a little effort anyone can tell them apart.

I've been duck watching in a couple of spots this winter, both favorites of more accomplished birders: the Piermont pier, which juts into the Hudson River in Rockland County, and the Edwin B. Forsythe National Wildlife Refuge in southern New Jersey, the Brigantine division. Along the Piermont pier, when there was ice in the river earlier in the year, I saw buffleheads and goldeneyes, northern ducks that fly south for the winter. It warms the heart, if not the nose and fingers, to see birds that look on the New York region as a warm-weather retreat. And both were in breeding colors, the buffleheads with bright white head patches and the goldeneyes with shockingly yellow eyes with black–dot pupils.

Later I saw canvasbacks, and on a day in February when the wind was fierce I watched a couple of small rafts of ruddy ducks taking shelter in the lee of the pier on the south side. Their tails were up and their heads tucked in as they drifted in the water, rubber–ducky style. And I spent some time watching mallards. You can find mallards all around New York almost anywhere there is water. If you're throwing stale bread to a duck, it's probably a mallard. But just because they're common doesn't mean they aren't worth watching. The males are perfect examples of the duck penchant for extravagant, shameless colors.

"Look at that mallard as he floats on the lake; see his elevated head glittering with emerald green, his amber eyes glancing in the light!" That's John James Audubon in *The Birds of America* displaying his drakelike penchant for dressing up his observations with extravagant plumage. "See that drake, how he proudly shews, first the beauty of his silky head, then the brilliancy of his wing spots, and, with honeyed jabberings, discloses the warmth of his affection." Honeyed jabberings indeed.

But that was written in the first half of the nineteenth century. You could write like that in those days without getting in trouble. You could also shoot the birds you watched, and eat them. Audubon described not only the colors of ducks but also how they tasted. He thought young mallards afforded "delicate as well as savoury food."

The Piermont pier requires pedestrian birding unless you have a special permit for your car. There is no shooting allowed. Brigantine is more liberal. An eight-mile "wildlife drive" runs around the rectangular perimeter of a freshwater pool and a brackish-water pond created by dikes, with controlled water levels. You can take your coffee-filled thermos and spotting telescope along in your car and just roll down your window to look at birds. And for those who follow literally in the footsteps of Audubon and prefer to carry a shotgun when they pursue waterfowl, the refuge is occasionally closed to nonshooting visitors to allow hunters to shoot the proliferating Canada and snow geese.

At Brigantine, before I tackled the ponds, I started out with a half-mile walk through a salt marsh. It was warm and bright, and the marsh was full of little brown, or perhaps gray, birds. Unless I'm way off the mark, some of them were sparrows. As to the others, I wasn't sure. They could have been warblers. But then again they might have been vireos. There was one I thought I might be able to pin down because it had a splash of yellow on its rump, but when I paged through the field guide (I was using

Sibley's) all that happened was that I became awed by the diversity of nature and humbled by my own inability to make sense of it.

So I went after the ducks. In the West Pool I found one in my binoculars, looked at the gray body and black tail, looked at the book and back at the duck again. I repeated this pattern several times. It took me a while but eventually I identified the bird. It was a gadwall! In the East Pool I picked out another duck that looked similar. I watched it dabbling, then saw that it had a long tail and a delicate white slash on its neck. Aha! It was not a gadwall. It was a northern pintail!

I know this hardly seems worthy of exclamation points. But I don't care. There is a distinct predatory thrill in capturing the identity of a bird. It feels like hunting, except there's no dinner involved. I felt triumphant. It no longer mattered that I had been skunked in the marsh. I had prevailed on the ponds.

I felt so good that I took another crack at identifying the little brown-gray bird with the yellow rump. I looked at the list of birds that inhabit the refuge. There, among the thirty-eight species under "vireos–wood warblers," was "yellow-rumped warbler." I flipped to the index in my field guide and found the picture. It did indeed have a yellow rump. That was my bird; I'm sure of it.

Emily Dickinson was right. Hope is the thing with feathers. But it's not a "little bird" as she said, at least not for novice birders. It's a big bird, fat, colorful and, if you take Audubon's word for it, tasty. It's a duck.

•

James Gorman writes about nature and outdoor recreation for *The New York Times*. He is the author of *The Total Penguin* and *The Man with No Endorphins*.

Parking Lot Birds

An underappreciated habitat
deserves our attention

Kenn Kaufman

A friend of mine recently went off to study birds in the Caatinga, an arid and thorny region of northeastern Brazil. He told me it was a habitat that had been neglected by biologists. His project struck me as a worthy one, of course, but I pointed out to him that there was another important bird habitat, much closer to home, that biologists had overlooked at least as much: parking lots.

I don't know why this habitat has been so universally ignored by ornithologists. To be sure, it is not an endangered habitat at the moment; the total acreage of parking lots in North America is probably still increasing. So a study of parking lots in North America would not get any funding from the bird conservation groups. Not yet, anyway.

But what of the future? Someday soon (as any science-fiction fan knows) we'll be able to beam ourselves from place to place. At the push of a button, we will transform ourselves into electrical pulses and then transmit ourselves to another spot. (It's just one step of technology beyond the current fax machine. Already we can fax pieces of paper from place to place, and all we have to do is apply that science to living things—in other words, learn about the fax of life.) When that happens, people may not bother with cars anymore, except as status symbols. Why sit in traffic when you can just beam yourself home from work? With fewer cars there will be less reason for parking lots, and those old asphalt slabs may be plowed up and turned into forests. What will happen then to the birds that live in parking lots? We should start studying the problem now, before it turns into an emergency.

Parking lots near the beach, thronged with cars in summer, are not really deserted in the off-season. After the human crowds depart, crowds of gulls often move in, to rest on these broad, open expanses.

This is not just a phenomenon of the coast. Gulls foraging along the Mississippi in winter will leave the river to rest in parking lots in St. Louis. Gulls from southern Lake Michigan will fly several miles into Indiana, to my old hometown of South Bend, to rest on the parking lots of Notre Dame. There are even parking lots in far-inland places like Oklahoma or Utah that are favored by gulls at times.

To anyone who knows how raucous the gulls can be when they're feeding, the peaceful air of these resting flocks may come as a surprise. Bills pointing into the breeze, the gulls line up all facing the same direction. The flocks have an orderly pattern, as if they were subconsciously heeding the regular rows of painted white or yellow stripes that mark off the slots for cars. Ruffling their feathers, standing on one leg, preening, dozing, the gulls wile away the hours.

Of course, they will not rest for long. When the tide changes, or when the shift changes at the local garbage dump, or when some other kind of feeding opportunity presents itself, they will be off in a blizzard of wings. But for the moment, they are quiet. They are, in a sense, parked.

Naturally, gulls are not the only birds that occur in this unnatural habitat. Some songbird types are found there as well. Along the Pacific Coast, but only there, one species wins the prize as the prevailing small bird in parking lots: Brewer's blackbird.

This species was named after someone named Brewer—Thomas Brewer, a nineteenth-century Boston physician and ornithologist—and not just some guy who ran a brewery. I bring up this point only because someone once asked me if "brewer's blackbirds" like to drink beer. No, they don't. They're not hanging around the parking lot waiting for more suds from the brewery; they're waiting for tortilla chips and bagel crumbs.

That's one of the things that makes parking lot birding effective. While some birds, like gulls, sometimes regard these big expanses of concrete as no more than good places to rest, other birds come here for the feeding opportunities. And of course the opportunities vary with location. Apart from being a prime territory for resting gulls, for a site to be classified as an IBPL (Important Bird Parking Lot) it should be near a food source. The parking lot for a fast-food joint inevitably will offer better birding than the parking lot for a fabric store.

At any rate, whenever I visit the California coast, I'm always struck by the fact that Brewer's blackbirds are everywhere in the parking lots and on the sidewalks around shops and restaurants. The males, sharp, glossy, blue-black birds with staring pale eyes, and the females, softer gray with brown eyes, go stepping about among the cars and pedestrians, seeking crumbs left behind by the shoppers. It's impressive to see how unconcerned they are about the bustle of human activity. But another thing that impresses me is that Brewer's blackbirds are *not* major parking lot birds elsewhere. Although the species is widespread over the western two-thirds of the continent, I have not seen it dominating the parking lot scene anywhere else except along the coast.

It may be that, in other areas, Brewer's blackbirds are edged out of this prime habitat by other species. In Tucson, where I live, it is the great-tailed grackle that reigns as the king of the parking lot. These grackles are big birds: the males can be a foot and a half long if we count the tail, and we might as well. When they are flying, they look as if they might be dragged down out of the air by their long, heavy tails. Around parking lots, though, the great-tailed grackles spend more time walking than flying, and more time standing around than walking. While the males are loafing at the edges of the lot, they often give voice to a bizarre series of noises—creaking, grating, crashing, scraping noises, along with factory whistles and clicks and clanks. They have a mechanical sound, as if the birds feel right at home among all the motorized vehicles around them.

Great-tailed grackles normally have pale yellow eyes after they grow up. A few years ago, however, idly studying the grackles around a burger joint in Tucson, I noticed that a couple of them—apparently adults—had dark eyes and some missing feathers. This sparked my curiosity. In the time since, visiting the parking lots of numerous fast-food restaurants here, I have continued to see odd things in the appearance of various grackles. Some have the wrong eye color; some are missing most of the feathers on their heads; some have patches of white, or generally dull plumage. Many of these anomalies could have been caused by deficiencies in the diets of these birds. If you're sitting in the parking lot eating your lunch and notice that you're surrounded by scruffy and malnourished grackles, it might make you look at your french fries in a whole new light.

Not all birds seem to be affected in a bad way by eating human junk food. A few have been with us long enough to adapt, to thrive on such fare. The everyday house sparrow has probably been a satellite of human civilization for more than two thousand years, adapting to life around city-states of the Mediterranean region, following the Roman legions as they marched across Europe, and later hitching rides with colonists who went to other continents. In some ways, house sparrows are the perfect parking lot birds. They get along okay on the worst food we can dish out, and they are resourceful at finding their own food in parking lots as well.

Have you noticed that, when you're driving, the front end of your car may develop a collection of smashed dead insects? Well, the house sparrows have noticed that too.

Many times I've seen house sparrows fluttering around in front of parked cars, picking choice morsels from the still-warm radiators. Not only does your car help to gather insects for these birds, the hot engine cooks them too: baked beetles, roasted roaches, fried flies, and other delicacies.

House sparrows are not the only birds to take advantage of these meals on wheels. In desert regions, cactus wrens often do the same thing. Cactus wrens are just as inquisitive as other wrens, but they seem much less nervous than their relatives about coming out in the open. (Come to think of it, since they live in the desert, they're out in the open most of the time.) At various parks and recreation areas in the American Southwest, you can find cactus wrens working the parking lots, collecting their own entrance fees in the form of grilled insects.

If you come back to your car in the parking lot and find one of these little birds picking bugs off the radiator you might say something like, "Oh, how cute." But your reaction might be different—you might say things that would not be repeatable in polite company—if you happened to be in New Zealand and the bird picking things off your car were that parrot called the kea.

The kea is a very large and bulky parrot the color of muddy moss but with a flash of flame-red under the wings. Its bill has a very long, curved, pointed upper mandible, a feature that Captain Hook would have envied. And the kea makes full use of this bill.

I've heard it said that a typical pet parrot is like a two-year-old child with a can opener on its face. If that is so, then a flock of wild keas is like a gang of teenagers with chain saws on their faces. There is still some debate, in the high pastures of South Island, about whether or not keas actually kill sheep. Either way, there's no doubt that keas are very good at taking the sheep apart once they're dead. And keas are very good at taking other things apart as well.

Once while visiting a little-used parking lot at high elevation in the Fiordland area of southern New Zealand, I noticed a family that had just come back to find that their car had been vandalized. The windshield wipers were bent askew, with the softer parts ripped away, and most of the rubber molding had been pulled away from the edges of the windows. After assessing the damage, and cursing the likely culprits, the head of the family climbed into the car and slammed the door—and the windshield fell out onto the dash. Louder curses. The broken glass was angrily tossed into the trunk, and the family drove away. Meanwhile, down at the far end of the parking lot, three keas were studiously working on another car.

It may be that the easiest parking lot birds to get along with are those that simply rest there, like the gulls, rather than trying to garner anything edible from cars or littering humans. But I want to mention another kind of bird associated with parking lots, living above them, not on them.

Some parking lots are well lighted at night. Perhaps meant to deter thugs, the lights also attract insects—many kinds of moths and beetles and a host of other insects fly to the lights. This in itself is reason enough for a closet entomologist like myself to stop and check these lighted lots at night. But the insects in turn attract certain birds. Nighthawks, which feed on insects that they capture in graceful flight, are regular nighttime visitors to the airspace above these lighted areas. Many times, while out for walks at night, I have paused to watch the aerial ballet of nighthawks high above well-lit parking lots.

Once, while driving across Venezuela, I arrived after dark at a hotel in the middle of a town in arid country. The parking area was a large lot behind the hotel, fenced in and brightly lit for protection. I maneuvered the car into one of the few remaining spaces with the shouted aid of the young boy who was attending the lot. As I was heading toward the hotel, I noticed several lesser nighthawks foraging quietly overhead.

Unlike the common nighthawk, with its frequent buzzy *peent* calls, the lesser nighthawk is typically a silent bird. The dozen or so that were now overhead were flying in total silence, coursing back and forth with slow, buoyant wingbeats, seeming to float above the lights.

The parking lot attendant came up to see what was wrong, but when he saw that I was staring upward, he relaxed. With an angelic smile, he explained to me in Spanish. "Swallows," he said, pointing at the nighthawks. "It is a luxury of the hotel."

Right you are, I thought. Who cares what the bird is called, swallow or nighthawk or something else? We should consider it a luxury that there are still birds that live around the edges of our cities and built-up places, and even in—or above—our parking lots.

•

Kenn Kaufman is one of the country's best-known birders. The author of the Kaufman Focus Guides, *Lives of North American Birds*, and *Kingbird Highway*, he also writes a column for *Bird Watcher's Digest*.

Jazz on the Wing

The wonder of ravens at play

Ann Zwinger

I stood waiting at the La Paz airport in Baja California—for clearances to be filed, customs to be cleared, gas tanks to be filled, flight plans to be filed. For none of which was I responsible, and since I had no designated task, I was bored. Bored and, worse, annoyed, because allowing oneself to be bored ranks in my mind right up there as the Eighth Deadly Sin. A vicious, pushy wind mirrored my ill mood, a malevolent wind that spit sand in my eyes, snatched at my jacket, tied my hair in knots, and unsettled my disposition. I stood beneath a row of acacia trees (a useless windbreak) whose long, dangling seed pods rattled against each other in a mindless chatter. Snippets of dried stems and branches galloped across the tarmac. In the distance, dust devils spun upwards, dusty water spouts. The wind bursts even shifted the incoming planes roars. Objectively, on the Beaufort scale that wind ranged somewhere between a 5 and a 6. On my personal annoyance rating, it was off the scale.

A halyard whanged mindlessly against a flag pole. I walked over to it, thinking to stop its annoying clatter by winding it onto its cleat. As my eye followed the rope's line upwards, it was then that I saw them: a confusion of black wings spinning like whirligigs, attached to a gaggle of cavorting ravens twenty feet above me ("raven" was a safe identification since I knew crows only occur in the far northeastern corner of the peninsula). I stepped out into the full wind to watch them. Half a dozen or so ravens were conducting takeoffs and landings, continually changing places on the pole's high crosspiece that they used like a diving board, one raven sidling out to the end, dropping off into space, while an airborne one landed, wings scooping the wind, black legs extended, feet like grappling hooks, coming in as fast as a plane landing on a carrier and stopping just as abruptly. As each raven took off it plummeted a few feet, then lifted its wings to catch the wind and oriented to its speed and direction, before essaying every airplane maneuver imaginable—barrel rolls, Immelmans, outside loops, inside rolls, snap rolls, and hammerhead stalls. Stresses that would have snapped an airplane wing impeded them not.

The wind sometimes caught their flight feathers and separated them, like spoilers on an Airbus wing. Although disheveled feathers should have interrupted the airflow, their flight was unaffected. But once a bird landed, there was the work of flattening windblown feathers before taking off again. The complex quadrille continued seemingly with no end in sight, no weariness.

To my eye they carried exuberance in their wings. Theirs was a grand right and left called by the wind. I know anthropomorphism is a no-no for natural history writers, and I plead guilty: the sheer joyous abandon in their body language communicated to me an exuberant, cocky "see-what-I-can-do" showing off.

I stood there entranced albeit sand-blasted. To me their flight appeared quixotic, unpremeditated, haphazard, without focus or pattern, as well as risky and fabulously skillful. Sometimes they looked like black mops gliding into land on a few inches of perch, watching the one displaced doing its own triple jumps and flying camels. Yet the longer I watched I sensed that there was a pattern. They used the air like a choreographer uses the stage, trying out new steps and patterns within the space allotted, ending with an unholy tarantella done with incredible skill and panache. Or perhaps they were jazz musicians, flying the first few bars of a song straight and letting loose their own wild improvisations.

A respectable literature exists about the purposes of play in training the young of the species—lion and bear cubs, fox kits, falcons, kittens, etc., who learn speed and coordination that will help them hunt and capture their own food. But the ravens were not feeding. I suppose you could make a case that such vigorous flying resembles an aerobics class, a way of keeping in shape, strengthening, refining flying techniques. Why not? But there was another daredevil quality, smart-alecky kids on the corner, showing off their new skateboards, trying another new madness.

This seemed to me playing for play's sake, spinning aerial fandangos for the sheer pleasure of movement, engendered by a wind that spun and spiraled with them, a *pas de deux* for each tux-suited raven as it caught the wind and used it, sweeping in exuberant waltzes and cheeky jitterbugging. It is anthropomorphizing to make that judgement but I can only use the words I know and the vocabulary I have and the perceptions I've developed: to my eye, they were just plain *playing* every time they cast themselves at the wind.

I think I know purposeful play when I see it—the honking and squawking, the salaaming and neck-stretching of young albatross trying to get the right mating moves in the right sequence, the proper Victorian courting of mallards, the Mobius-looping flight of male broad-tailed hummingbirds, all the candy and flowers, all patterned and purposeful, with mating in mind. These birds were *not* playing in the frivolous sense, they were getting on with the main business of life: reproduction.

There's good reason to use the word "play." Bernd Heinrich, who knows ravens as well as anyone, and whose books have enriched scientific and natural history reading, devotes a whole chapter to play in *Mind of the Raven*. People are always sending him "raven play" stories, about ravens hanging upside down from branches or power lines, frolicking in the updrafts along a high cliff, flying with gliders, sliding down roofs, hanging by their bills, queuing up along the ridge of a sand bar where they position themselves in sequence to be lifted off by a gentle wind that sets each down again, only to rise and set down again. Heinrich acknowledges that play is part of their education because ravens "act out neural patterns that have evolved to be internally rewarding, because those individuals that are proximally rewarded in behaviors that ultimately benefit them engage in them more, survive, and leave more offspring." I can buy into that survival-of-the-fittest idea, but I like it best when he refuses to "indulge in endless speculation on the ultimate benefit that these many kinds of play could have to ravens. Your guess is as good as mine. There are few data to prove or disprove almost any hypothesis we might come up with." That puts me firmly on familiar shaky ground.

I have not again seen such willful, frivolous, spectacular bird behavior. After more than thirty years, a windy day often evokes the vivid memory of those ravens, black as patent leather, just having the best time imaginable. The picture that sweeps back into my mind is still fresh and still gives me, in recalling their verve and élan, a sense of their joy in living that parallels mine. I shall not forget that glorious free-for-all abandon, that birling and swirling, their lyrical surfing on the waves of the wind.

•

Ann Zwinger is the author of numerous books on the natural world, including *Shaped by Wind and Water*, *Downcanyon*, *The Mysterious Lands*, and *Run, River, Run*, winner of the John Burroughs Medal for nature writing in 1976. She lives in Colorado.

To Drink from a River, to Swim in the Milky Way

A miraculous river of raptors
flows over Veracruz

Clay Sutton

I am alone on the hotel roof, the first time I have been alone for over a week. That's why I mounted the stairs to the sixth-floor rooftop hawk-watch before seven o'clock. I am seeking quiet time for contemplation and perspective.

The vista is a study in gray, the rain-laden gulf clouds hanging low over the ocean to the east, blocking the morning sun and muting the verdant tropical tones. Pico de Orizaba, Mexico's highest peak, nearly seventy-five miles to the west, is visible, though, its snow-covered slopes bathed in sunlight and shining through the humid coastal clouds. The volcano is distant, dormant, but dominant. It brings to mind prehistoric days, when nature more visibly controlled our planet. It's only the second time I've seen the mighty mountain, and I wonder if it could be an omen, a portent of good fortune for the last day of our tour.

I discover I have company. The local peregrine, probably wintering here now, sits atop the radio tower across
the street, nearly eye level and scope-close. I see it preen,
then sleepily close its eyes, dreaming perhaps of its arctic
aerie or maybe fat Latin pigeons. A Yellow-throated
Warbler forages in a palm tree in the city park below,
seemingly way out of place to one who is more used to
seeing Yellow-throated Warblers on their now-distant
breeding grounds, in the pines at Jakes Landing, just a few
miles from my New Jersey home.

The city of Cardel, Veracruz, is slowly rousing. The
smells begin to drift up, invisible tendrils wafting over the
parapet, a uniquely tropical blend of wood-fire smoke, fry-
ing foods, fresh produce, and pastries. Later in the day, the
Latino bustle—noise, music, horns, unmuffled engines—
may perhaps be hard to reconcile with the tranquil beauty of the farmlands and sugarcane fields beyond the city,
but now, early, it all blends together into a background
hum easy on the mind. On transmission towers beyond
the edge of town, Black Vultures and spread-wing Turkey
Vultures festoon the girders, awaiting the sun, or thermals,
or perhaps just waiting.

The sky is blue to the west, but a cloud bank hovers
in the east, threatening. The wind is from the south; the air
seems to be thickening. Being from the east coast of the

United States, I automatically assume there needs to be a northwest wind to trigger fall raptor migration. I begin to fret. Will they come today? Almost all of the world's Broad-winged Hawks pass over Cardel, but the big flight hasn't occurred yet. It's overdue. It's October 3, prime time, indeed *peak* time, but for me, for us, it's now or never—today is our last day here, the final day of our bird tour. We missed the big flight last year. Will that happen again? If so, it won't be "you should have been here yesterday" but "you should have been here tomorrow."

The city fully awakens. Cars and trucks loaded with people ply the streets below. Volkswagen taxis whiz around in all directions. Bus horns blare. The birds awaken, too. Red-billed Pigeons streak over, a small flock of Aztec Parakeets clatters by. Noisy, grating Great-tailed Grackles litter the town square. The sad calls of caged birds filter up from beneath red tile roofs.

The first kettle is right overhead, low, point-blank, although I somehow never see it coming. About fifty Broad-winged Hawks and nearly thirty Swainson's Hawks—more Swainson's than we've seen all week, a good sign. Scanning reveals flocks forming, hawks getting up out of the trees, swirling low to the north of town. Will it happen? Is it happening? Please, please, please . . .

Now the flocks, though still small, are advancing, coming on and over as steady as the waves on the nearby beach. As rising morning thermals falter, the birds stream, heading due south, streaming in legions, looking for the next kettle forming over an altitude-gaining thermal. For a broadwing, migration is deceptively simple: convert altitude to speed, speed to distance—distance that stretches from Canada to South American cloud forests.

I am no longer alone. The hawk-counters arrive and comment on how early the flight has begun. They speculate that this might be "the big one." The official count begins at nine, and such is the scale, the enormity, of the Veracruz flight that there is little concern that the counters might have already missed maybe a thousand birds.

The distant waiting vultures stir, flapping, struggling initially, then locking their wings and joining the whirling uplifted kettle. The sun breaks through, the lambent light cutting the humid haze to reveal kettles stretching to the western horizon, to the base of the hills that constrict the flyway. Our group and others arrive on the roof and marvel, some loudly, some quietly and personally. I scan 360 degrees and do a quick count. I estimate that 22,000 broadwings are now in sight at once. A veteran raptor biologist tells me that my guess is too low.

The miraculous flight begins to shift inland as the south wind turns east, causing the flocks and lingering clouds to drift away from the coast and our rooftop vantage point. We hastily arrange to move. When we hit the street, the city din crashes like thunder. I realize, dumbly, that it wasn't that we hadn't heard it, couldn't hear it, six flights up, but that the clamor had simply disappeared, fallen away while we were lost in the world above. I recall one time in southeastern Arizona's "sky island" mountains when fog and clouds cloaked the vast valleys below, the peaks becoming islands in an ocean of mist. This was similar, the hotel rooftop a quiet island in the roiling sea below. As we board the taxis, above the noise I hear the still-perched peregrine chatter a challenge at another passing Peregrine Falcon as it rushes by, streaking south.

We race inland, trying to get back underneath the flow, arriving at Chichicaxtle, eleven kilometers inland, about fifteen minutes later. The town of "Chichi" is the auxiliary count site, used when gulf-effect east winds push flights west of the Hotel Bienvenido and downtown Cardel. We erupt from the cars onto a schoolyard soccer field, dodging not only soccer balls, but a gamboling, galloping donkey, too. Looking up, we are awed, dumbstruck. Broadwings now stretch from horizon to horizon, from the east from whence we came to as far west as we can see.

The advancing streams of birds extend back into infinity against the blue cloud-shrouded hills in the north.

I begin to realize that despite twenty-five years of hawk-watching I am unprepared for this event. I have seen several flights of maybe 10,000 broadwings in Texas and enjoyed at least two 10,000-plus days at Cape May. And the previous year, we witnessed a 149,000-hawk day at Cardel. But that flight had been high, protracted—manageable.

I am now hard-pressed to comprehend the enormity, the magnitude of this passage. It defies logic. I have always been able to enumerate, to pigeonhole, a flight, but now I am simply overwhelmed. The hawk-counters, mostly silent under the pressure of the siege, nevertheless take the time to tell us "We just counted twenty thousand in sight at once." Twenty thousand. More than an entire season at most major hawk-watches, a lifetime's supply at lesser ones. Accordingly, there is little to measure the Cardel flight by, no yardstick that works.

So we don't even try to count. We just watch, awestruck, looking up in open-mouthed wonder at the incomprehensible journey above. With writing in mind, I try to think of ways to describe it. But it's like trying to photograph the Grand Canyon—largely impossible. I have a passing thought of a living, moving erector set, for each kettle is connected to others by streams of hawks, a vast matrix high overhead, like a sky-full of molecular diagrams.

The vast streams converge and coalesce, coagulating into kettles. The birds then circle endlessly, gradually rising. Finally, as the thermal dies, they stream again, heading for the next signpost, a kettle marking a column of upward-flowing air. The kettles themselves are vast vortices, torna-does of hawks snaking up into the sky. Because the clouds have remained, most birds are silhouettes, yet all are low. The counters would later say that it is rare, indeed almost unique, to have such a big flight so low, so point-blank overhead. The birds may not be struggling, but because of the cloud cover, warmth and resultant thermal lift is pre-cious, and the birds spend an inordinate amount of time circling before streaming south. The kettles are like pitch-ers filling with water. The level rises from the bottom, over-flowing the top when the pitcher can hold no more. I focus on a specific point in the middle of a kettle without moving my binoculars. It's like looking through a child's kaleidoscope at a shifting, swirling pattern of raptors.

As the blizzard of birds covers the sky, we marvel, yet in the way of humans, or at least biologists, we try to describe it. Tom Wood, here with his wife, Sheri Williamson, both on busmen's holidays from their jobs as codirectors of the Southeastern Arizona Bird Observatory, says it best: "It's like looking at a galaxy of hawks, a Milky Way of birds." Indeed stargazing is the only time in my life I have seen so many objects in the sky.

It's soon past noon, and the passage continues. We are almost giddy now. Ridiculous thoughts come. I laughingly wonder if the team of counters ever needs oil for their clickers or to throw water on them to cool them off. Then I'm troubled by the thought that they might develop carpal tunnel syndrome from the clicking. Raptor-induced CTS. One broadwing flies upstream, resolutely flapping north. What's up with that? Sheri quips, "He forgot his keys." As a particularly low and orderly group of hawks skims by, Sheri says, "God, I love a parade!"

The pageant continues unabated. Our Pronatura colleagues (from the dedicated premier Mexican conservation group, who study, count, and protect the migration) have termed the world's largest hawk flight *El Rio de Rapaches*, "The River of Raptors." I now understand why. Flocks of birds stretch from horizon to horizon as they come from the north and flow to the south. The river is now cresting, overflowing its banks. It's at flood stage.

Mid-afternoon. The clouds continue, but it is the warmest part of a tropical day. Some hawks are in high streams, traveling much farther between kettles. There is more time to appreciate the variety. High Ospreys, wings set, push south. Here a Cooper's Hawk, there an American Kestrel, yonder several Mississippi Kites. A high Zone-tailed Hawk masquerades among the Turkey Vultures, and a paddle-winged Hook-billed Kite contrasts sweetly with the slender Swainson's and Broad-winged hawks.

The afternoon brings a push of waterbirds. Flocks of Wood Storks appear, mostly in loose Vs, flapping more than soaring. Distant gooselike strings materialize into vast flocks of White Pelicans, first wheeling in unison, flashing brilliant white against blue-gray skies, then peeling off into ever-changing lines as the strings cross. It's as if they are trying to spell out something in a language not yet learned, a cipher understood only by pelicans. Overhead, lines of Anhingas, gangly, prehistoric, glide silently amongst the broadwings.

It's close to three P.M., and the flight endures un-checked. After seven hours, the movement has become almost mind-numbing. At one point I become disorient-ed, spatially confused by all the converging, diverging flocks. The discomfiture leads to a temporal drift; the mag-nificent journey in the sky harkens back to earlier times, to a less embroiled, threatened earth, a primal planet. I experience an overwhelming sensation that this is the way it should be, a conviction that this is right. I try to shake off the disorientation; I attribute it to lack of sleep, a hectic schedule, the end of a long tour. I try to refocus but then realize that it is more than that; deep feelings are welling up.

I walk off, leaving the group, and wander over to the other side of the now-quiet soccer field. As a raptor enthusiast, I had always wanted to see "the big flight," to experience not only the river but a flood. I had always wondered how long it would take, how many years, if ever. I had come so close so many times, at Hawk Mountain, Santa Ana, Duluth, Braddock Bay. The realization that this was *it* hit hard; the drama of the life above sobered me. I stood apart, and tears filled my eyes. It wasn't so much that I couldn't speak, I just couldn't think of the words. It was the first time in my life I'd ever walked away from a tour I was leading, but at that moment I needed to be alone.

Back home in New Jersey, I'm an active naturalist, plying the woods a fair share of the time, probably more than most. This summer past I knew of just two local pairs of broadwings, and the thousand or so that pass Cape May each year are but a trickle, a tiny tributary to the raptor river flowing over Veracruz. That more than 1.7 million broadwings pass over Cardel each fall is more than a spectacle, it's a miracle, a testament. It shows just how vast the eastern North American forests are—so large that they can produce this unfathomable number of broadwings. Such thoughts are restorative: that the United States and Canada can still produce this vast wealth of creatures at the top of the food chain, that South America can still absorb and nurture them in winter as our northern forests sleep. There is a message of hope in this massive broadwing flight. As long as there is a pure and free-flowing river of raptors, maybe the problems of the planet are not insurmountable. Maybe at least there's still time.

Much later that evening, after hours of compilation, the Pronatura hawk-counters relax in the Hotel Bienvenido's street-side cafe, drinking celebratory *cervezas*. The sound of a gentle tropical rain mixes with mariachi music, muting the drone of the traffic. The biologists give us the news: the official count for the day is nearly 500,000 broadwings. They also say that the flight was so large and broad-fronted that they probably missed at least part of it. It boggles the mind to know that they have had single-day counts of over one million birds at Cardel, Veracruz. It is incomprehensible to imagine a flight twice as large as that day's.

I've not seen the great bison herds on the American plains as they moved beneath endless flocks of Passenger Pigeons darkening prairie skies. Nor has anyone in our time. Nor will anyone ever again. It will take another planet, another heaven and earth, for that to occur. I have never seen the great plains of the Serengeti, and I have yet to see the enormous seabird flights above the Bering Sea. I hope to, someday. But I have been privileged to see green Mexican mountains turn orange with winter Monarch Butterflies, and I've shared the arctic tundra with vast herds of Caribou migrating across the north slope of Alaska's magnificent Brooks Range. And now I've quenched my thirst for hawks, nourished by the River of Raptors that flows uninterrupted down Veracruz's lush coast. These visions speak to me, to us, of what the Passenger Pigeons must have been like in their multitudes. They are visions of the past, and yet of a possible future. In Veracruz, immersed in a swirl of hawks, I now know what it's like to drink from a river and to swim in the Milky Way.

•

Clay Sutton is a lifelong resident of the Cape May region. He is the coauthor of *Hawks in Flight, How to Spot an Owl, How to Spot Hawks & Eagles,* and *How to Spot Butterflies* and regularly leads birding and natural history workshops and tours near and far.

Take Me to Your Sewage Lagoon

Intrepid Mississippians know
where to find the best birds

Judith A. Toups

Wherever we live, we birders find it increasingly difficult to locate places that attract birds and are at the same time amenable to the activity of birding. We scratch this or that former little hot spot from a time-honored birding route and wonder where to go next. Perhaps we should expand our collective birding mind-set to include some places where we never would have thought to look.

The local source of effluvia is a fact of life, and even though it represents burgeoning development and diminishing habitat, it could be a birder's best bet for finding water in an asphalt desert, and therefore, some very classy birds. Up for your consideration: the local sewage lagoon.

Some decades past, simple logic worked well for a desperate upstate Mississippi birder who tired of making two-hour drives to coastal counties to see his ration of birds of watery persuasion. So he studied a map of his own land-locked community until he found the county waste-water treatment plant, which came to be known among birders as the Hattiesburg sewage ponds.

His first forays to the ponds were met with resistance from county workers, and the view from outside the chain-link fence was woefully inadequate. But his frequent presence on the far side of the fence eventually led those with an "in" to trust that his motives were pure and his methods benign. He was given a release form to sign, a key to the gate, and leave to drive around the plant's four huge ponds. He had found his own utopia, and it was just down the road from home. Naturally, word spread.

Larry Gates and the Hattiesburg ponds soon became famous. Larry's contributions to the state's dossier on wildlife included first state records and, more importantly, a number of first inland records of species long believed to be in absentia. The ponds themselves became a regular destination for birders within a short driving distance, and a priority stop for birders heading north to Memphis or south to Biloxi along U.S. 49.

Those ponds in Hattiesburg, smack in the middle of the Pine Belt, where birds are somewhat predictable, changed the attitudes and opened the minds of dozens of birders, who began a run on similar places all over the state. Not only did the Hattiesburg ponds yield prize birds, such as Red Phalarope (an oceangoing shorebird) in 1977 and Red-necked Grebe (a first state record) in 1978, they absolutely teemed with ducks and other waterbirds in winter and during migration, as well as shorebirds on the sludgy banks, sparrows and pipits on the perimeters, and, in spring and fall, colorful songbirds in the vegetated surroundings. Thus they gave hope to every birder whose own fiefdom was under siege by land-grabbers at the gate.

So the generic wastewater treatment plant was fulfilling a need other than that for which it was intended; it was serving as a wildlife refuge, where shooting was illegal, where traffic and road noise were minimal, where the back-to-nature crowd, boom-boxes attached, would not be caught dead, and where none but a paid employee would willfully enter.

In our own birding bailiwick, we took a page from Larry's book and gathered vital intelligence. In Hancock County, on the coast, we learned of the Waveland–Bay St. Louis Wastewater Treatment District, which, when seen through the fence, was one big pond, a sleepy-lagoon sort of place, parklike and rather inviting from a distance, surrounded by a negotiable dirt road, its entire perimeter lined with bramble, brush, bushes, and trees of great variety.

As treatment plants go, this one was hardly state of the art, and it would eventually fall into the "auxiliary" category. When we first visited, no one was present and there was no on-site office, thus no one of whom we could request admittance. But the view through the fence, and the thought of the site's potential for birds, raised the ante on what we would do to gain entrée. For several weeks, we drove to a road behind the lagoon and squeezed through a pre-existing hole in the fence—furtive, frustrating birding. The pond, even when scrutinized from hiding places in the vegetation, was chock-full of birds, everything from big, showy egrets, ducks, and other waterbirds to shorebirds plying the edges, wrens in the sedges, and warblers in the trees.

Eventually we were nailed by two workers in a pick-up truck. They had the authority to escort us to the gate, and to mend the fence, but they did neither. Instead, we talked birds. They were innately knowledgeable, in a good ole boy, lived-here-all-my-life way, about what lived and loitered at the lagoon. And they wanted to know if we had seen the alligators; they were very proud of their alligators (which suggested that there was a watery access route somewhere nearby; in fact, years later, these two great guys invited me into a putt-putt boat and we actually slurped our way around the lagoon and out to a couple of center "islands," where gators loafed between meals).

They were more than willing to share the keys to the kingdom of what came to be known as the Waveland Lagoon (capitals, please). Our immense gratitude took the form of homemade cookies, and, to strengthen our foothold, we provided a used field guide and later, a copy of *Birds and Birding on the Mississippi Coast*, in which they were rightfully acknowledged. It's been an amicable relationship, and the good fallout from it has lasted for many years, during which the birding contingent has been accepted and welcomed, though not necessarily understood, at Waveland.

And the birds! In the first eight years of birding Waveland, we learned that more than two hundred species had also found the place. There were enough locally rare birds to sustain a legend: Eared Grebe, Surf Scoter, Black Scoter, Common Merganser, Merlin, Peregrine Falcon, Vermilion Flycatcher, Scissor-tailed Flycatcher, Western Kingbird, Groove-billed Ani. And then there were additions: Cinnamon Teal, Roseate Spoonbill, Ash-throated Flycatcher. In a relatively short period of time, the lagoon proved to be the best single-spot birding in all of Hancock County, Mississippi. Even though our original intention was to find water and birds with links to water, the lagoons and their surrounds were equally attractive to land birds, what we call songbirds, or even postcard birds. The rarest species (because it was well out of range) we ever saw at the Waveland Lagoon was a Painted Redstart that came front and center out of a sea of migrating American Redstarts in October 1989.

All these attention-getters notwithstanding, the most spectacular birding I ever experienced anywhere within North America came inside the gates of the Waveland Lagoon in November 1985, and it involved almost every birder's most coveted group of birds: the wood-warblers.

It was the year when a capricious hurricane named Juan danced and dallied up and down the coasts of Mississippi and Louisiana for about five days in late October. Its threats were real, and it was doing costly damage to crops and the fishing industry, but Juan was gentle enough, as a tropical storm, to encourage a few intrepid birders to seek out the birds that such storms are wont to produce (mostly oceangoing species). As Juan gave up its ghost on October 31, a Thursday, we were out scouting in anticipation of a weekend meeting of the Mississippi Ornithological Society.

Except for a few out-of-season Black Terns, there wasn't a single unexpected species at the Waveland Lagoon, where the birding had been good all during fall migration. The transient warblers and tangers and buntings had all but cleared out in mid-October, and it was a little too early for the winter ducks and sparrows. A rainy cold front began its passage the next day, and clouds and mist were to continue into Saturday. The forecast almost dashed our hopes for successful birding.

During the meeting, my role was to lead a group to the lagoon. I did not have many takers—there was a barely explored catfish farm up the road (a new world to conquer) and the beachfront to satisfy upstate birders who were looking for coastal species. Undaunted, our small group entered the lagoon area early Saturday morning. Almost immediately, we encountered no fewer than forty Black-throated Green Warblers in some yaupon bushes just inside; unconcerned with us, they were feeding on berries, furiously, as if they had just flown out of a charter bus at a Burger King. The amazing thing was that they hadn't been there yesterday, or even a week ago.

Our adrenaline rushed us from bush to bush and tree to tree. Twenty-eight species of warblers had convened in the vegetation, including a record of about three hundred Bay-breasted Warblers (in any given year we would hardly hold out hope for one after the third week of October).

But it was the twenty-odd Cape May Warblers that put the day onto an existential plane. We just don't see Cape Mays in Mississippi in the fall. Even in a "good" year, a birder could rest on the laurels of having seen just one misguided Cape May Warbler. The ramifications of that warbler windfall were astounding. We were seeing birds, some of them long past their "normal" departure dates— unexpected ones, like the Cape Mays, or unknown, like the Blackpoll Warbler—that could not be passed off as late-stayers or confused vagrants.

I'm not sure when the term "reverse migration" came into the picture, but the phenomenon seems to have been exemplified by the events of that weekend. When weather systems collide, anything can happen, and November 1 and 2, 1985, prove it. Those two days at the Waveland Lagoon also crown my collective years of indelible birding experiences.

Another memorable experience: not long after the Waveland Lagoon had made it into the "fabled" ranks, I was hired to escort a group of not-a-hair-out-of-place socialites on a Waveland birding excursion; their priority was to see some of the birds I had been writing about. The outing was to double as a birthday celebration for one of them, so lunch and a birthday cake were on the agenda. Reader, even though I have eaten such goodies as shrimp salad followed by cream puffs in the well-ventilated confines of my own car, I had never, before or since, sat on the ground next to a linen tablecloth reaching for my share of hors d'oeuvres and dainty little finger-sandwiches and drinking champagne from a crystal flute all while hearing the echo of a cement-bunkered pump resounding with the combined flushes of an entire city work force home for lunch.

At about the same time that the Waveland Lagoon went down in the record books, another more modern facility was being completed in Ocean Springs, Jackson County (also on the coast). It consisted of three ponds, around which were negotiable roads, and a magnificent view of open spray fields to the north. It was a scant distance from Interstate 10 and five minutes, on a good day, from downtown Ocean Springs.

It is now familiarly known to birders as the Seaman Road Lagoons. We could not wait to get in there, but officialdom thought otherwise, at least for a time. From a vantage point outside the fence we could see enough assorted ducks to suggest just the tip of a gigantic iceberg (picture a chocoholic looking through the window of a candy store that is closed for the weekend). We are not easily dissuaded from getting to where the birds are, or might be, and it is worth mentioning the following suggestions for the benefit of those who seek access to their own version of the Seaman Road Lagoons.

Go to, or write to, the person, or the managing body, in charge. State your case thoroughly. It helps to do so under the aegis of an "official" bird club, Audubon chapter, ornithological society, or even an institution of higher learning. Litanize what tried-and-true or rare and exotic species might be found there. Mention the growing lack of "natural" birding areas. Emphasize that there are precedents, that many cities, counties, states, and even foreign countries put out the welcome mat for birders at treatment plants, outfalls, and similar hallmarks of contemporary progress. Note that birders have put such facilities as those in Willcox, Arizona (for shorebirds), Baltimore, Maryland (where a Ross's Gull once lingered), and Eilat, Israel (where bird-tourism has flourished), on the birding map. Offer to compile a bird list; we live in an age when bureaucracy parades that which hints at environmental awareness. Suggest a sign-in, sign-out sheet. Be nonconfrontational but persistent.

That is how we came to learn that the Seaman Road Lagoons is the best place for birds in Jackson County, Mississippi. Eared Grebes, lots of 'em in fall and winter, do not seem to know that they are in the eastern United States; their annual presence at many lagoons suggests a latent preference for such places. Roseate Spoonbills and Wood Storks stop by. Upwards of seventy-five Mississippi Kites have soared overhead during migration. Purple Gallinules and Least Bitterns are prolific in spring and summer. Shorebirds of assorted ilk, even Sanderlings, find an alternative to disappearing natural mud-flats and recreational beaches. Ducks drop in for a day and stay for the winter. Rails call from the man-made marshes, and sparrows and open-country birds flush from the spray fields.

The appeal of sewage lagoons to birds and therefore to birders may be incomprehensible to those who wouldn't say "sewage" in polite company. After years of looking at the birds that haunt these putrid ponds, it has become clear to me that while certain species that rarely visit this state may have proclivities for larger bodies of fresh and salt water in their regular venues, they make a beeline for this state's waste repositories. All but one of the Red Phalaropes ever seen in Mississippi were eyeballed at sewage lagoons. Likewise, birds such as Red-throated Loons; Eared, Western, and Red-necked grebes; even sea ducks such as Long-tailed Ducks and the scoters are more commonly, or at least as often, seen in such environs instead of in the harbors and bays of the Mississippi Sound, or in the state's freshwater lakes.

The rarest of the rare birds ever found at one of Mississippi's lagoons? That's easy, and a story unto itself. Terry Schiefer, an entomologist at Mississippi State University in Starkville and a birder of note, was determined to make

1992 a banner year for his annual state list. Maybe because of that, he frequently visited a humble sewage pond that, to most of us, had been lost in the shuffle; it was in Oktibbeha County, just a few trifling miles outside of the university town. He was there on a cloudy, cold, and thoroughly uninviting January 31. And he was in a most unenviable spot for a birder with a bell-ringer of a bird in binocular view: he was alone.

It was past bedtime when my hot line sounded at home. Terry had found a Yellow Wagtail! Forget the usual inquisition—the questions one birder would ask another when roused from a sound sleep by an excited voice announcing a mind-blowing fine-feathered find—Terry Schiefer is not the sort to lay false claim to a bird that, in North America, breeds only in Alaska and makes infrequent appearances only along the Pacific Coast. It takes approximately five hours on the highway to get from coastal Mississippi to Oktibbeha County. Nothing but a five-alarm bird could get most birders out of warm beds and into the cold night, but at least two car loads of midnight riders from the coastal counties took the bait and were wandering around the outskirts of Starkville just after dawn on February 1.

Terry was leaving nothing to chance. Like directions to a garage sale, signs saying "Wagtail" were tacked to posts and fences all along the route, and soon we Mississippians were part of a gathering that included birders from Alabama, Georgia, and Tennessee. Terry was in the middle of it, but all eyes, bins, and scopes were on a two-bit yellow bird mincing in and out of the cattails. We ooh'd and aah'd, checked field guides, and aimed cameras while the little lost bird cooperated to the fullest extent of its capabilities. That it was a wagtail was elementary.

Sometime within the next couple of hours of scrutiny, however, a suggestion was made by Greg Jackson, an Alabama birder of high repute. He opened a field guide to the birds of Europe (no one else had thought to bring one), flipped to the wagtails, and began making a case for a bird most of us had never heard of—a Citrine Wagtail, which breeds in far eastern Europe and had never been seen in the Western Hemisphere. (Greg had visited Europe as recently as the past summer. If memory serves me, I was the only birder there who had at that time ever seen a Yellow Wagtail, that being in Nome, Alaska, where a North American variety of the Yellow Wagtail rightfully belongs.) Certainty wavered. Confusion reigned.

We left Terry and his wagtail with judgment pending. As if it wouldn't play to an empty house, the wagtail departed sometime during the afternoon and was not seen again. Terry sent a bundle of photos to Europe's high-echelon birders, and they concluded that the bird was indeed a Citrine Wagtail. Soon thereafter, the Mississippi Ornithological Society's Bird Records Committee included the species on the official state bird list. That same Citrine Wagtail also made it into the pages of Kenn Kaufman's *Lives of North American Birds* (1996) with the accompanying remark "wagtails are known to be capable of straying long distances." *The Sibley Guide to Birds* (2000), on the other hand, makes no reference to it.

The records committee of the American Birding Association and the American Ornithologists' Union later accepted the Citrine Wagtail—and that was good enough for me. By any name it was the rarest bird ever to be seen in Mississippi, and the rarest bird I have ever seen anywhere.

In recent years, the perverse path of progress has rendered the Starkville Sewage Lagoon unfit for habitation by birds of any ilk; to drive home that point, No Trespassing and Keep Out signs are prominent. Fortunately, such prohibitions are the exception and not the rule.

My list of high-priority birding places begins with our sewage lagoons. During the three decades, give or take, that they have become known and appreciated for their secondary roles as bird havens and hangouts, the state list of birds has taken a quantum leap. Because we are aware that the lagoons are there, and worthy of being birded on a regular basis, we are constantly learning more about the true status and distribution of much of our avifauna.

As the lore of sewage lagoons has spread, so have the number of birders who visit them. Perusal of the sign-in sheet at almost any wastewater treatment facility is an eye-opener; in Mississippi, lagoon birder-visitors have come from all the lower forty-eight as well as Canada, and some from afar—across the big pond to the east. We have learned, or are learning, where to look; we know that for every crowded city park, boat-filled lake, littered picnic area, and bikini-clad-nymphet–strewn beach, there is a quiet pond, lagoon, or treatment plant that isn't listed under "points of interest." And amen to that.

•

Judith A. Toups is coauthor of the landmark guidebook *Birds and Birding on the Mississippi Coast*. She lives along the Mississippi Sound.

The Best Birding in Lincoln

Wilderness thrives in a
forgotten corner of the city

Paul A. Johnsgard

A city the size of Lincoln, Nebraska, with nearly 200,000 people, is one in which birdwatching locations within the city limits basically boil down to only a few options: backyards, city parks, cemeteries, and recovering dump grounds. Backyard birds are little different in Lincoln than from anywhere else in the Midwest, although in the past few years, house finches have to a considerable degree replaced house sparrows at feeders, common grackles have become even more common, and greater numbers of usually migratory species such as mourning doves have been overwintering, aided in part by warmer winter temperatures and increased numbers of bird feeders. But northern cardinals and blue jays tend to rule the roost at local feeders.

Occasionally we have some "good" species migrating over town at great heights: flocks of snow geese, Canada geese, greater white-fronted geese, and, rarely, marbled godwits and long-billed curlews. One of my previous graduate students has done periodic bird-banding in the backyard of his landlord's house. Over several years he has banded twenty-six species of birds there. The list of birds seen in the yard or flying above it is now at about fifty-six species.

The city parks within Lincoln are mostly the usual highly manicured type, without a great deal to recommend them ornithologically except for some small lakes. Recently, I ate my lunch beside one such lake, Oak Lake. It was an early and cloudy October day with occasional rain squalls. There were dozens of Canada geese on the lake, a lone immature pied-billed grebe floating aimlessly about, and flock after flock of barn swallows overhead, pausing only briefly to grab tiny insects from near the water's surface as they scurried southward. They were behind schedule and should have been gone before the end of September. Later that week a thousand or more Franklin's gulls visited the lake briefly, also on their way southward. But the smell of winter was in the air, and the usual summer sounds of western kingbirds, house wrens, warbling vireos, and overhead cliff swallows were lacking. A flock of American avocets briefly touched down the following week.

Outside the city limits are two much larger city parks: Wilderness Park, with a riverine hardwood forest lining a small river, and Pioneer's Park, with remnant areas of native tallgrass prairie. Both offer attractions at different seasons. The 1,400-acre Wilderness Park has a bird list of 191 species, including 33 warblers, 20 sparrows, 12 hawks, 4 owls, and 6 shorebirds. It is the best place for warblers and other neotropical migrants in the spring and has a few species that are near or at the western limits of their Nebraska breeding ranges, such as tufted titmouse and Carolina wren. Scarlet tanagers and summer tanagers are among the most memorable birds I have seen there. The 680-acre Pioneer's Park has several lagoons, other more natural marshy wetlands, and a small creek passing through it. It is older, more developed, and has more diverse habitats than Wilderness Park. Its bird list has 237 species, including 28 shorebirds, 28 warblers, 21 sparrows, 10 hawks, and 5 owls.

We also have several cemeteries in Lincoln, of which by far the best for birding is the oldest. Wyuka Cemetery was established at the time Lincoln was founded, just after the Civil War. As a result, it has some great oaks and other trees dating back more than a century. There is also a very small drainageway passing through it, where shrubs and weeds fight a valiant battle against herbicides and power lawn-mowers. Here too warblers congregate in early May, and migratory sparrows cluster in search of seeds and insects.

There is also a hike-bike trail, the MoPac East, that begins in central Lincoln and extends east about thirty miles along an abandoned right-of-way of the Missouri-Pacific Railroad. The right-of-way encompasses about 350 acres and has a bird list of 120 species, including 20 warblers, 18 sparrows, and 11 species of the blackbird family. When walking it one always has to be on the alert for speeding bikes, so it is not my favorite birding location.

For those with an even greater roving tendency, a drive to Omaha's two major nature preserves, Neal Woods and Fontenelle Forest, make the chances for spring warbler sightings even better. Both are situated along the Missouri River, a major north-south flyway for neotropical migrants. Fontenelle Forest has a bird list of 246 species, and that of Neal Woods is 190, with several wonderful and rare warblers such as yellow-throated, parula, prothonotary, and cerulean among their attractions.

But of all these many areas, one of Lincoln's greatest ornithological gems is in my opinion its dump ground. More accurately, it is the old city landfill, which after much of a century finally became too filled with the city's castoffs to be maintained, and furthermore the city was expanding to its very borders. Thus, in the 1990s, much of it was abandoned, and a new landfill operation began farther away from town. Luckily, it was abandoned before the native habitats had been completely destroyed. The original landfill's edges graded off into a marshy wetland traditionally called Roper's Lake, which was apparently deemed unfillable. In the early 1900s, this area was evidently one of the best wetlands in the vicinity for hunting waterfowl, but such activities were terminated when the city limits were expanded to include the entire area south of Salt Creek.

The waters here, as well as the creek running through Lincoln, are distinctly salty, thus the name Salt Creek. This saltiness exists because instead of being deeply covered with glacial drift, a layer of Dakota sandstone comes close to the soil surface locally. Its porous materials are laced with salts that were deposited in it when the entire area was part of a vast inland sea several hundred million years ago. Nearly all these saline wetlands around Lincoln have recently been filled in, diluted with freshwater runoff, contaminated by herbicides and pesticides, or otherwise destroyed. By the time Lincoln administrators realized the rarity of these wetlands, and some of the equally rare plants and insects they support, it was too late to save most of them.

It was some years after I moved to Lincoln that I discovered this site, by poring over old city maps in search of wetland habitats where I could take my ornithology class. Seeing "Roper's Lake" on older city maps, in an area identified on more recent ones only as a landfill operation largely off-limits to the general public, made me want to investigate. There is no access from the north or west, as Salt Creek forms the landfill's northern and western boundaries, and from the east there are no roads. This left only the south, through the gated entrance to the landfill.

My first efforts to get in were rebuffed. I was told I could enter only to drop off materials for the landfill and if I paid an associated fee. After checking with city officials, I learned that I had a right as a citizen to enter the area for purposes other than dropping off lawn clippings or similar wastes. All that was needed was a show of determination at the gate, a pair of binoculars and a field guide to prove innocent intent, and a willingness to drive over what at times were some pretty badly rutted roads. I was, however, warned that there might be hazardous materials there, and that walking over the surface could result in falling into holes where rusted containers had collapsed belowground.

From the first time I visited the area, it was clear that this was indeed the premier birding site in Lincoln. A pair of resident great horned owls lived in an earthen cavity along Salt Creek, coyotes were common, and a herd of at least thirty deer occupied the woodlands. There is always at least one pair of red-tailed hawks to be seen, as well as many American crows. In recent years the one-time lake has become transformed into a shallow marsh that is now mostly overgrown with cattails and rushes, but it still sometimes attracts spring flocks of several hundred snow, white-fronted, and Canada geese, as well as gadwalls, green-winged teal, pintails, and other dabbling ducks. Red-winged blackbirds are there in the hundreds, and yellow-headed blackbirds in the dozens, the latter a species that is quite rare in eastern Nebraska. Most recently, great-tailed grackles have been seen in small numbers and are likely to colonize the wetland. During some springs a flock of black-crowned night-herons has stopped for a time, but they have never remained to nest, and Canada geese always stake out their territorial claims early. Each year I expect to see or hear rails. I am sure soras and Virginia rails at least are there, although I have not yet encountered them.

Almost every year the landfill offers up new surprises. In the fall and winter it attracts American tree sparrows, Harris's sparrows, and once even some longspurs. On one recent Christmas count we recorded nineteen red-tailed hawks and three northern harriers in the landfill area and its immediate vicinity. Early spring brings waterfowl, sometimes including relative rarities such as cinnamon teal. Flocks of larger migrating shorebirds such as whimbrels and godwits sometimes fly overhead, as do ospreys and migrant hawks that supplement the resident red-tails and American kestrels.

During late April shorebirds such as yellowlegs and semipalmated plovers can be seen along the shorelines and bars of Salt Creek, and once during an ornithology field trip I saw a single western grebe floating down the stream. In order to get ahead of it and make it turn back toward the class, I took off in a full-speed run, only to fall into one of the unexpected holes I had been warned about. Fortunately, I didn't break any bones.

One of the attractive features of the landfill is that scarcely any other birders are aware of it, or, if they are, they don't make the effort to get beyond the gate. Thus, unlike in our city parks, there is no one riding through on mountain bicycles, no fishermen, no teenagers with blaring boom-boxes, and little noise of any kind, save for the voices of nature. Although I have taken nearly every ornithology class I have ever taught to the site, only a few people have come to love the place as much as I do. Here one can often see bullsnakes, garter snakes, and other smaller, less conspicuous snakes such as the woods-loving brown snake. Bullfrogs and other frogs fill the late spring air with incessant sound, and summer brings cicada choruses. Here too any footprints of canines one sees in the dust are more likely to be those of coyotes than domestic dogs.

During late summer and fall the place is especially beautiful. I recently went there on a mid-autumn day, when the trees were at their maximum color and the prairie grasses glistened with golden, copper, and bronzy tones. The sky was October blue, with some wispy clouds telling me that colder weather was not far away. The ring-billed gulls evidently believed the clouds; several flocks passed over and headed southward without even stopping to see what sorts of foods might be present on the land-fill. Shortly after arriving I saw a herd of white-tailed deer in the distance, all walking toward me at a leisurely pace. I stopped in my tracks and watched as they approached sin-gle file. An adult female was at the front, a mixture of eight likely females and juvenile males in the middle, and a well-antlered male took up the rear. The lead female was only about fifty feet away when she finally detected me. With a snort she wheeled about and, with tail erect, headed into the tall marsh grasses, closely followed by all the rest.

Soon I came upon the sun-bleached skeleton of a dead tree, well riddled with woodpecker cavities and

insect holes. A pair of eastern bluebirds and a single youngster were actively investigating every crack and cranny,
paying little attention to my presence. Not far away were
several wild plum thickets, now nearly leafless and exposing several bird nests of the previous summer. More than
twenty sparrows, mostly Harris's, with a few white-throats
and a party-busting eastern towhee, sat comfortably within, the group occasionally exchanging one thicket for
another for no apparent reason. But winter was obviously
not far away. Garter snakes were moving slowly, and the
grasshoppers were making only half-hearted jumps to get
out of my way as I walked along.

In May, the place is alive with birds and bird song.
Because of the large amount of woody edge, consisting of
riverine shoreline and forest, and woods-grassland edge
around the wetlands, there is a terrific variety of songbirds
that like woody borders and open woodlands, including
orchard orioles, rose-breasted grosbeaks, least flycatchers,
and blue jays. Indigo buntings sing from the woody edges,
and northern orioles build nests in the taller cottonwoods.
The marsh is a cacophony of red-winged and yellow-
headed blackbirds, with song sparrows and common yel-
lowthroats adding their opinions from the rushy sidelines.
On such a morning one can expect to see forty or fifty
species quite easily. For me, walking through it seems

something like walking through the Garden of Eden, proving that beauty can take root and thrive, even over the refuse of humankind.

•

Paul A. Johnsgard is the author of many books on birds, including *Prairie Birds*, *North American Owls*, *Pheasants of the World*, and *Hawks, Eagles, and Falcons of North America*. He teaches at the University of Nebraska.

The Birds of Tikal

A patient birdwatcher finds treasure
amid Mayan ruins

Lawrence Kilham

When traveling in Central America in winter in the 1970s, my wife, Jane, and I sought places where we could live reasonably and see wildlife from the doorstep or in unspoiled forest close at hand. The nearest we came to our El Dorado, and a place we visited three times, was Tikal, in Guatemala. I had generally found Lineated Woodpeckers, which are much like our Pileateds, a shy species and difficult to watch in Central American rain forests. But at Tikal, by the Mayan ruins, I found several nests that were ideal for watching. A pair of Lineateds that nested by Temple 2 were so habituated to people that they paid little attention to us. We climbed to the plaza every morning early, carrying box breakfasts so that we could watch at the best hours of the day. It was always exciting when the sun first struck the ruins. Few people came before ten o'clock, and we had the plaza, the temples, and the Lineateds more or less to ourselves before then.

Temple 2 at one end of the plaza, and the Jaguar Temple at the other, rise stepwise and clifflike. The birds that dominated the ruins, for those who had an eye for them, were a pair of Orange-breasted Falcons. One could almost always see one on a dead limb rising above the southwest corner of the plaza by Temple 2.

Busy watching Lineateds, I was slow to realize what an unusual opportunity I was missing with the falcons. Two things about them slowly dawned on me. One was that I could climb the ruined temples to where I could watch them at thirty feet, and another, that these falcons were rare in Central America and, until recently, had almost never been studied. But it was not until February 8, 1978, that I was roused to turn aside, for a time, from the Lineateds. This was when the male Orange-breasted, the tiercel, giving cries and with a rush of wings, landed right above me. He was bearing a robin-sized bird in his talons, and small feathers were soon floating in the wind as he plucked it. The falcon was so beautiful that I felt I must climb for a closer look. When I arrived at the top of the temple I was able to see the falcon within thirty feet and at his own level.

The view from the top was magnificent. Ruins of temples lay in one direction, the forest canopy in others. The tiercel continued plucking his prey for twenty minutes, then, giving single cries, flew with it over the plaza and back. He rested a few moments with the prey in his bill, then flew to his mate perched on a tree above where I sat. She had been waiting for him with feathers ruffed. She took the nearly plucked carcass from him and, holding it in one foot, tore into it with quick pulls of her hooked bill. The view of these two beautiful birds at close range was unforgettable. At only twenty feet, they filled the whole field of my binoculars. I could scarcely have been closer. The feet and bill of the male glistened with the blood and juices of his victim.

I now slid into an alcove shaded from the sun to watch the female. Downy feathers clung to her bill as she continued to feed. The prey was small, but it took many nibbles to consume. What a magnificent bird she was! Although the male Orange-breasted Falcon is a third smaller than the female, both have the same plumage— blue-black above, with bright rufous breasts merging into white throats.

The female took wing after fifteen minutes, making the plaza resound with shrill *ca-ca-ca*'s that synchronized with her wing-beats. She never went far on her flights. Like falcons of other species at the time of egg-laying, she spent much of her time on only a few perches, letting her mate bring food to her.

On the following morning the female falcon began giving *chup* calls, crouching flat with head down and wings out as her mate flew to her. He then mounted, giving loud cries as mating took place. The more I watched, the more amazed I was by how noisy the falcons were. Once attuned to their cries, I was continually aware of them, even when they were at a distance.

There is no accounting for tastes. During our three visits to Tikal hundreds of birders went through on Audubon bird tours, checking off species under guidance of a leader. None that passed seemed interested in looking at any bird at any length. Those birders that we talked to regarded it as queer that we should spend two or three weeks a year at what to us was a naturalist's paradise when it was well known in their circles that one could "do" Tikal in a few days.

It was while watching miscellaneous birds at Tikal that Jane and I saw four Crested Guans, large, dark-colored game birds, come to an open limb at eye level and only thirty feet away. They had hardly landed when they exploded in four directions. What had happened?

Jane had seen a hawk fly among them. All I knew was that one of the guans was screaming bloody murder. The sounds were mingled with growls. Could the guan have been caught by an ocelot or jaguar? Excited, yet fearful that I might be seen and spoil everything, I crept along the edge of the plateau we were on, hoping to catch a glimpse. I found that the guan making the screams was unharmed. The same bird was also making the growls. My jaguar was a fantasy. The guan suddenly flew toward me into the center of a tree with the hawk in pursuit. The hawk, stopped by the tree's outer branches, clung with wings beating and tail outspread. I could now see that it was an Ornate Hawk-Eagle.

The guan switched to *cawk, cawk, cawk* notes at a rate of 144 a minute as soon as the hawk left. Then, with crest raised and the red dewlap of its throat showing, it began to preen.

How to account for the wild outburst of vocalizations? Much has been written about the alarm calls of birds. Some think that the caller is exposing itself for the good of its fellows. This noble idea kindled my thinking on the guans, not because I agreed with it, but because I saw things differently. Predators, it seems to me, succeed by coming upon their prey unawares. Imagine the effect, then, of the guans, a prey species, breaking into a barrage of screams and growls that are among the loudest and most dramatic sounds one is likely to hear in neotropical forests. Only the howls of howler monkeys are more formidable. Might not such an outburst disconcert a predator such as an Ornate Hawk-Eagle—enough, at any rate, to make it fumble an attack?

There was another element to the guan's outburst that might also have had an effect. The jaguarlike growls fooled me. Might they not also have fooled the hawk-eagle, at least momentarily? I can well imagine the hawk-eagle thinking, "Could there be a big cat in there? Might it not be better to clear out?"

Rails, of kinds I am familiar with in the north, live among reeds and, being nocturnal, are difficult to see. This was true of the comparatively large Gray-necked Wood-Rails we found when we first went to Tikal. Even if I rose at dawn, all I saw of them by the *aguadas*, or small reservoirs, was a glimpse of one disappearing for the day. The next year, however, the wood-rails were staying out for several hours, and by our third year, having become accustomed to the number of people passing by the *aguadas* daily, they were as tame as domestic fowl, five of them running over the lawns that surrounded the reed beds. Here, with the lawns enabling me to move about, was an unusual opportunity for watching an unusual bird. Sitting in one place, then another, I found the wood-rails, with plumages so smooth as to appear almost featherless, beautiful birds to watch. Their pattern of colors—bright rufous on their bodies, blue-gray necks, and jet black under rear ends and tails, plus yellow bills and sturdy red legs—was striking at close range.

The rails fed largely on pond snails. But one afternoon one of them caught a water snake about a foot long and ran away with it writhing in its bill as two other rails pursued. The captor had to keep running to retain its prize. Once at a distance, it put the snake down, rained blows on it, picked it up, shook it, and pounded some more. But the snake was a tough one and seemed to be unsubduable. It was still able to rise, open its mouth, and face its tormentor after twenty-five minutes. If the rail had no appetite to begin with, it must have had one by the time it made its first attempt at swallowing the snake ten minutes later. This first attempt got the snake halfway down—but not for long. With more writhing the snake gained its freedom, only to receive more blows, shakings, and poundings. The rail tried to swallow the snake five more times without success. Then on a seventh attempt, the snake disappeared headfirst down the rail's gullet, leaving only a few inches of tail hanging out. Downing these last few inches was a hard go. But finally, after a total of forty-five minutes of wrangling, the snake disappeared within the wood-rail. Would the rail now take a rest? Contrary to expectations, and looking as though nothing unusual had happened, the wood-rail resumed looking for pond snails.

The reason I was able to watch this normally shy bird so long and in such detail was its tameness. Wherever I travel I always regard tame or relatively tame "wild" birds as bonanzas for watching. The opportunity of watching such shy birds as Gray-necked Wood-Rails might be hard to duplicate. I could imagine going to Tikal just to study them alone. What an *embarras de richesse* was there! I not only enjoyed my wood-rails but found out later that neither snakes nor pond snails had been described in their diets. They may have found other food as well. I watched them enter a Guatemalan hut one morning and, jumping up on the table, poke around among the cups and dishes.

Out beyond what we called the "Indian Village" at Tikal lay a long, lonely track, barely a road, that ran to the distant ruins of Uaxatun. The road was at its wildest when Jane and I took walks there on late afternoons. Some distance out there was a muddy stretch with pools of water in deeper ruts. This was hardly a place where you would expect to see one of the more beautiful sights among birds. Yet it was to these dark pools, we found, that a Purple-crowned Fairy, a large and beautiful hummingbird, came to bathe at the approach of evening.

The water in one of these pools was settled and clear one evening when a Purple-crowned Fairy hovered above the water at the closest range of our field glasses. Held upright and almost stationary by its rapidly beating wings, it faced one direction, then another, as if to assure itself that all was safe. I could see, in these moments, every detail of its plumage, from bright purple crown with jet black through the eye, to snow-white belly, long outer tail feathers, and green-gold on the back. After a minute of hovering, the hummer plunged vertically into the pool, sending up splashes of water with each plunge. It was an exquisite ballet, played in the last rays of the sun.

Jane and I continued to walk along the track in the gathering dusk. We soon became aware of strange grunting noises that seemed to be all about us. By what creatures were we surrounded? Suddenly a group of about twenty peccaries, all massed together, came out on the road ahead of us. I could not see them well. Could they be White-lipped Peccaries? A frightening thought, as White-lippeds have been known to chase hunters up trees and keep them there all night. I soon saw, to my relief, that the peccaries had the bands of lighter bristles around the neck of Collared Peccaries. It was a bit scary, nonetheless, to find ourselves in the midst of a herd of them chomping in thickets all around us in the dusk.

Night comes on rapidly in the tropics. We had to walk fast, right on through the peccaries, to get back while we could still see our way. It was in the last fading light that we heard Great Tinamous, a bird somewhat like a small guinea fowl (although no relation), answering one another in the forest. Their haunting, flutelike notes are among the most beautiful ones to be heard in the neotropics. By this time we had reached the Indian Village and were close to the *cabana* where we stayed.

One of the many attractions to behavior watching is that it ties you to a place long enough to let you really get the feel of it. And one way to get such a feel, as we found on the lonely road to Uaxatun, is to be out as night comes on.

•

Lawrence Kilham is the author of *The American Crow and the Common Raven* and *On Watching Birds*, which was awarded the John Burroughs Medal for nature writing in 1989.

Parallel Worlds

A hummer, a hawk, and a house cat meet in a Tucson backyard

Kenn Kaufman

O ur house is small, but it has a second floor, an unusual arrangement here in Tucson, where one-story dwellings are the rule. I have always wondered whether my wife, Lynn, favored this house because of the stairs—because, as an inveterate cat-lover, she knew that a carpeted stairway was the perfect romping area for kittens. Mookie, our current cat (or, I should say, Lynn's cat), is far past kittenhood, but he still finds occasion to dash madly up or down the stairs several times a day, proving the point.

At his small size, shifting between floors has to be an adventure, a move on a grander scale than it would be for a full-sized human. And I suppose Mookie needs the diversion. He's an indoor cat: in our neighborhood, out-door cats are soon eaten by the local coyotes (and Lynn stonily rejects all my suggestions that we should send the

Mookster outside to play). So his predatory exploits are limited to nabbing the occasional cricket in the living room. For entertainment he romps on the stairs, or sits at the windows for hours to watch the happenings outdoors, his own personal movie of the larger world.

One morning I was coming down the stairs, at a slower and calmer pace than the cat would have used, when a movement outside the back window caught my eye. Mookie was crouched at the window, tense and alert, staring out. Halting in midstep, I stared as well: a hummingbird was hovering just outside the glass.

This is Tucson. There are always hummingbirds around, of several kinds, every day of the year. Most other places are not so blessed, I know, so I make a conscious effort not to take the hummers for granted; after seeing them frequently throughout the day for many years, however, it becomes all too easy to glance at them and mentally tick off the species represented—"Yes, it's an Anna's; yes, it's a blackchin"—without pausing for a longer look. But on this morning I froze on the stairs, because I recognized this hummingbird, really recognized it. Not just as a Costa's hummingbird (which it was), but as an individual.

Costa's hummingbirds are desert creatures. Most hummingbirds tend to avoid the desert, and with good reason:

they feed on nectar from flowers, a source that is often hard to find in this arid country. In such an environment of scarcity, Costa's cope by staying mobile. They seek out arroyos and hillsides where the shrubs bear small flowers that most of us would miss, moving on when the flowers run out, surviving on tiny insects as they seek another patch of blooms. They may vanish from big sections of their range for much of the year, not migrating north and south but performing some sort of east-west movement that is poorly understood. Tough little nomads, they wander in search of survival.

Around the edges of some cities in the Southwest there are places where hummer life is easier, places where natural desert life lies next to tended flowerbeds, with blooms available most of the time, and scattered hummingbird feeders to take up the slack. We happen to live in such a spot.

The row of small backyards down our block stands against a natural desert hillside. There are Costa's hummingbirds here almost all the time, and I have sometimes imagined that I was recognizing the same individuals over long periods, but I never could be certain.

Then this one showed up in the neighborhood: an aberrant bird, a partial albino. It was clearly an adult male Costa's hummingbird, with its purple cap and purple flaring points of feathers at the side of the neck, but it had an irregular white patch on its greenish back—like no other Costa's I'd seen. Suddenly, of all the anonymous mass of hummingbirds, one wore a badge of identity.

Intrigued, I started keeping track of this Costa's. I would prowl the neighborhood and the nearby desert at different times of day to seek him out. Every time I found him he was within two hundred yards of our back door, even though I searched farther afield. It seemed like a very small home range for a bird that could fly so fast—ten minutes, and he could have been miles away—but perhaps it was all the space he needed. Costa's are among our smallest hummingbirds, and this one was feeding at flowers that were small as well. He might spend five minutes working all the little blooms of the salvia plants low along the edge of the house before suddenly darting up in the air, a whole five feet over the wall into an adjacent yard, disappearing for the next hour.

This bird had several favored perches, high twigs at the tops of dead branches on mesquite or palo verde trees, with unobstructed views in all directions. I would see him on these high posts, his shoulders hunched in an aggressive posture, his head twitching from side to side as he scanned the area constantly. He would dart out to visit flowers, dart out again after any passing hummingbird, whether it was another male or a female—looking for food, looking for a fight, looking for a date. He was a hopped-up midget with a giant chip on his shoulder, a hyperactive tyke on a perpetual sugar high, the ruler of his miniature world.

Seeing this bird as an individual, day after day, I experienced a shift in outlook: for the first time, I really imagined that I could see things from the viewpoint of a hummingbird. It was a startling perspective.

Lynn's little garden plants suddenly loomed as giants: towering eighteen-inch spikes of penstemon, the vast jungle of a calliandra bush. When the Costa's took one of his high perches on a desert tree, he was as high, proportionately, as a grown man standing atop a fifty-story building. Not that he would have cared about the comparison to grown men. Although he would visit our hummingbird feeder occasionally (with the same studied aloofness as Mookie approaching his food dish), I had the feeling that we humans did not even register with him—we were just too big and too slow to matter. Although we inhabited some of the same space, the hummingbird and I were really living in two different worlds.

Then one day this bird disappeared. For more than a year he was absent, and during that time more generic, anonymous Costa's hummingbirds filtered through the neighborhood. Now, suddenly, he was back. From where I stood on the stairs, there was no mistaking that odd white patch on his back. For a moment I was just as excited as Mookie the Cat seemed to be.

But as I watched, there was sudden excitement of a different sort. A burst of action in the backyard. Frantic finches flying in all directions, two of them thumping into the window before turning and fleeing.

A split second later, the cause of the panic became obvious as a young Cooper's hawk swooped in to land on a low branch.

Cooper's hawks are forest creatures, at least over most of their range, hunters that lurk among dense treetops. In the desert around Tucson they might seem to be singularly out of place. Indeed, in true desert areas they are mostly lacking, limited to the narrow stands of tall cottonwoods along rivers. But Tucson is no longer true desert: its square miles of suburbia now have many planted trees, including out-of-place things like tall eucalyptus and pines, and Cooper's hawks have moved into town. There are now many nesting pairs in Tucson, even near the heart of the city.

I have lived here off and on for more than twenty years and have enjoyed watching these stealthy hawks infiltrate the city. Most Tucson residents probably fail to notice them altogether, but alert birders see Cooper's hawks regularly, all over town. In a typical sighting, the hawk appears abruptly, flapping and power-gliding low and fast across the street, barely clearing the top of a fence to vanish into a hidden backyard; seconds later comes the explosion of panicked doves or grackles, fleeing in all directions. Sometimes a Cooper's will perch boldly atop a pole in the open (as if it imagined itself to be a red-tailed hawk), but if disturbed it is likely to seek cover immediately in one of the tall trees thoughtfully provided by its human neighbors.

Several times over the years I have followed the progress of nesting pairs, but my most vivid impression of their lives came vicariously. A pair of Cooper's hawks built a nest in a tall eucalyptus tree near the offices at the Tucson Botanical Gardens, where Lynn is (among other things) the resident bird expert. The entire staff of the gardens took pride in hosting these hawks and took note of all they did, and as a result Lynn was able to give me a complete hawk update every night. So I heard about the edgy courtship of these high-strung raptors, the circling and displaying with the potential for violence just below the surface. I heard about how the male would bring food to the incubating female—not to the nest itself but to an Aleppo pine nearby, where the female would dart over to snatch the offering from her smaller mate and bolt it down. I heard about the long period when everyone wondered whether the two young in the nest would ever, in fact, learn to fly. Whenever I stopped by the gardens myself, I knew the context for any observations of the moment.

The hawks were pointed out proudly to visitors to the gardens, achieving a certain degree of fame in the community, and ultimately they were enlisted to aid the cause of science. Researchers from the local university had been studying urban Cooper's hawks (one of the parents at this nest had been banded by them earlier, at another site), and they came to make observations here as well. They even attached a tiny radio transmitter to one of the young hawks about the time it was learning to fly.

As the young hawks became independent and all the members of the family began ranging more widely, I gradually heard less about them, and eventually the hawk updates ceased entirely. I had not even thought about these birds for a couple of months until one day when Lynn mentioned that she had heard from the university researchers. The radio-tagged young Cooper's was still being tracked, and it was still in the Tucson area, but it had moved a dozen miles southwest of its birthplace—it was now ranging around the edge of town, near the old San Xavier Mission.

For some reason, that fragment of news captured my imagination. I began to picture the city from the viewpoint of the young hawk. This city would be just ordinary habitat for a hawk that had been born here, a habitat with a lot of wasted space (streets, houses, parking lots) but with enough trees for cover and enough slow-witted sparrows, grackles, and pigeons for effective hunting. From thirty or forty feet up in the air, the grid of the city would be laid out in a map of clear signs: green patches of shelter, dangerous lanes of heavy traffic to be avoided. Other hawks would be apparent from up here, too: other Cooper's hawks, a few Harris's hawks, aggressive predators that might not tolerate newcomers. So the young Cooper's had kept moving, drifting into new neighborhoods and being chased out again, going hungry on those days when its hunting skills proved not quite well developed yet, but always learning. And always seeing this city from the air, in ways that I could only imagine. From its aerial perspective, humans would have been irrelevant, just another species dwelling in the same habitat: too big to eat, too earthbound to be interesting.

All of this flashed through my mind as I stood on the stairs. The hummingbird had not yet fled like the finches when the hawk arrived. It still hovered there, looking at the hawk (too slow to be a threat) while the hawk looked at it (too small to be worth any effort), and I looked at both of them, along with the cat in the window. For a moment it was like an alignment of planets, as if our four different worlds were intersecting.

The moment was brief. Then the hawk flew, swooping low over the back wall. Seconds later the hummingbird flashed away in the opposite direction. Released from the spell of the moment, I walked on down the stairs.

Mookie had not moved. He was still crouched at the window, quivering with tension, his tail twitching back and forth. "Stupid cat," I muttered (ignoring the irony of mentioning stupidity when I was, in fact, speaking English to a cat), "the birds are gone. Haven't you noticed?"

He didn't budge at the sound of my voice, so I walked over to the window and looked where he was looking. Inches away from his nose, just on the other side of the glass, a cricket was crawling along the window ledge.

•

Kenn Kaufman also contributed "Parking Lot Birds" to this collection.

A Man for All Seasons

Thanks to his father,
a son notices the birds

John Nichols

I live in a small house in Taos, New Mexico. From my kitchen doorway I look across a narrow strip of garden to a storage shed where I keep many books and file cabinets. Nailed high on the far edge of this prosaic structure is a nesting box for starlings. It's two feet tall, six inches wide, eight inches deep. The entrance hole up top has a two-and-a-half-inch diameter. The roof boasts a three-inch overhang. The box was once painted light umber but is now simple weathered wood, covered in front by bird droppings. My dad built it for me twenty-six years ago, and birds have nested in it every year since.

The box has been through my three marriages and three different locations. It has been nailed to silver-leafed poplars, Chinese elms, and my storage shed. Cats, ravens, and magpies have attacked it to no avail. It is a professional starling box made by a professional birder (who's also a good carpenter). My dad knew what he was doing.

His name is David Gelston Nichols. He is eighty-one years old and lives in Smithville, Texas, a small town forty-two miles southeast of Austin. As long as I have known him he has taught me about wildlife, especially birds. His father, my namesake John T. Nichols, was a distinguished naturalist and for many years curator of fishes at the American Museum of Natural History, in New York City. From him my father learned much about tanagers, sticklebacks, spiders—the fantastic web of life. To me he passed on a naturalist's awe and curiosity.

When my mother died, shortly after my second birthday, Pop went off to the Second World War. I lived with cousins in Smithtown, New York, on Long Island. From the Solomon Islands Dad sent letters to me and his father in which he drew us pictures of frigatebirds, butterflies, wild pigs, bats, lizards, cardinal lories, monkeys, and "white pigeons with green backs and red knobs on their bills" sitting in banyan trees. Perhaps that is when I became irrevocably hooked on nature.

I did not truly meet my dad until after the war, in 1945. My fondest memories are of being with him at his family's summer home in Mastic Beach, on the south shore of Long Island, the old William Floyd estate. His mother, Cornelia Floyd, was descended directly from

William Floyd, who signed the Declaration of Independence for New York State. The house was a simple colonial structure surrounded by 613 acres of fields and forests and salt meadows leading to Moriches Bay. In 1965 the family gave the whole place to the U.S. government. It is currently a museum and wildlife refuge, part of the Fire Island National Seashore.

We found box turtles at Mastic and marked them, keeping a record for decades. Dad gathered mice and other animals for the museum of natural history's small-mammal collection. I followed him on his morning rounds of checking traps and watched as he prepared museum specimens on the kitchen table. He explained their habits and told me their Latin names. It excited me enormously to see those critters up close.

From behind the Mastic shutters my father plucked little brown bats, unafraid to handle them with his bare hands. He called my attention to woodcocks towering at dusk above the front field. He could identify any bird nest, whether it belonged to a flycatcher, a phoebe, or a sparrow. If a thing warbled or chirped or cried out of sight, Dad knew whether it was a towhee, a red-eyed vireo, a green heron, or a herring gull. His veneration of those beings gave him great status in my eyes, and even before I could read I was an environmentalist.

Dad encouraged me to have leaf collections, to learn the names of butterflies, to be fascinated by praying mantis eggs. I kept frogs in terrariums and an occasional painted turtle in the bathtub. We observed dragonflies and darning needles and paddled over sunfish nests. He lifted a snapping turtle by the tail. With bamboo poles we fished for flounder and snapper blues, while gulls and dozens of other birds flapped overhead. He gave names to all things that crawled or swam or soared, telling me where they wintered and how they raised their young. Even ticks and sand fleas and deer mice belonged to a priceless habitat.

All his life my father observed birds, from primitive blinds, through one-way windows in the house, and from cabins and mountain perches and boats and automobiles. He took thousands of bird photographs that today are kept neatly, carefully annotated, in dozens of looseleaf albums. Though a number of blinds were lost as he moved around, that never slowed him down: new camouflage boxes and bunkers and cabanas instantly arose in fresh territories.

When I was seven he tried to carry a large, flimsy blind on a canoe from Indian Point at Mastic over to an island in Moriches Bay. He dumped the box in five feet of water but eventually lugged it to a beach. I have snapshots of him setting decoys in the sand. Using a Graflex camera he photographed the birds attracted by the decoys. I crouched in the blind with him as he took pictures of sanderlings, plovers, dowitchers, and perhaps a laughing gull.

We often walked along the beach at Fire Island. There was wind in the dune grasses and least terns darting about our heads and sandpipers skittering alongside the foamy ocean wavelets. We inspected horseshoe crabs lolling in the surf. I collected crinkly black skate eggs, hoarding them like priceless treasures. Everything was presented to me as an important part of the universe.

In later years we went out with a sensitive Uher 4000 recorder, capturing bird songs on tape. Afterwards, Pop slowed down the tape so I could hear the higher-frequency notes, which were inaudible to us until they were altered in this manner. At reduced speed, the melodious complexity of a meadowlark's song was compounded, outdoing anything invented by Mozart or Beethoven. I was mesmerized by the intricate tonalities of bird language.

My father is a big, tall man who has always worn a crew cut. He's a serious intellectual and a professional scientist. He has a lusty sense of humor and laughs a lot about sex and human folly. He has run traplines in Nevada and observed the behavior of pelicans at Port Aransas, Texas (1997), and Miami, Florida (1942). A crab spider he discovered in Cantwell, Alaska, on August 15, 1937, was named after him: *Xysticus nicholsi*. He earned a Ph.D. in psycholinguistics at age fifty at the University of California, Berkeley, and taught for twenty years at the University of Colorado at Colorado Springs: comparative animal behavior, communication of emotion, human survival, and even some courses in statistics. He speaks fluent Russian and French and enough Chinese to raise a couple of guffaws at a good party. Nobody can play the guitar and sing "Little Joe the Wrangler" better than David Gelston Nichols. A risqué limerick pops out of his mouth for virtually any occasion. And he once told me this: "John, the trouble with empirical science today is that scientists pretend make-believe is unreal."

Pop grew up hunting and had a true aim—he liked the taste of squirrel. But in his early twenties he abruptly quit blood sports, and then wrote a poem about his change of heart. Here are the last three verses:

> The light of day is fading
> And far out on the lake
> The hen duck glides as yesterday
> Alongside of the drake.
>
> They float there close together
> Safe and free as air.

I held my trigger finger.
I could have had the pair.

When they move on tomorrow
Those birds belong to me.
I had a chance . . . to hold . . . or kill,
And chose to set them free.

My grandfather gave my dad his first pair of field glasses in 1925, when Pop was nine. He used the glasses in the Solomons and in China. He used them on flamingos in Florida, on pipits and grizzlies in Alaska, on avocets in Berkeley's Aquatic Park. He also trained his binoculars on crows attacking a great horned owl in Rock Creek Park in Washington, D.C. I know, because I was there.

It happened in 1956. The old man has always talked with crows. He caws to them and listens to their answers and makes a passel of notes. In Rock Creek Park he had a pole with a stuffed owl affixed to a crossbar on top. He stuck the pole in the ground, marshaled me under a tree, and cawed up a storm. Inside ten minutes two dozen birds were noisily mobbing that owl. I was properly astounded.

Pop's curiosity extends to most anything in life. He's interested in religion and has long been involved with Psychologists for Social Responsibility. He is active in the

Bastrop County Environmental Network. His concern for the environment runs deep. He writes a column called Nichols' Niche for the weekly *Smithville Times*. Topics for the Niche have ranged from the proper disposal of road-kill to his thoughts on worldwide conflict resolution. In print he has pondered computer languages, biofeedback, ring-billed gulls, the endangered Houston toad, censorship and pornography, mourning dove threat posturing, the psychology of cults, and the meaning of good-luck pennies found on the ground. (In pocket-size notebooks he has kept a record of every penny that he's picked up since 1960. He faithfully records his thoughts at the moment of discovery. Whenever I find a penny on the ground, I think of my father.)

Twice we drove across the United States together. In the winter of 1950 we traveled from Berkeley to Washington, D.C., in an old Studebaker loaded with suitcases, a parakeet, and a Siamese cat named Boris Caleb Cadwallader. He gambled for me in Reno; we slid off the road on ice in Colorado, almost tipping over. The old man kept a record of bird life along the way. In Kansas we clobbered a ring-necked pheasant. Pop slammed on the brakes, went into reverse, and threw that pheasant in the trunk, where it promptly froze. We ate it on our second night back east.

In 1978 we hit the road in tandem again, from Colorado Springs to Long Island to bury my grandmother. By now my father had a tape recorder on the front seat of his Chevy Impala, and he kept interrupting our conversation to remark on the bird life. "Two grackles at one o'clock . . ." "One kestrel on a telephone wire . . ." "Three turkey vultures feeding on a mound of bloody fur, probably a skunk . . ." He did that all the way across.

Pop tells me he became a serious birder as a small child, participating in Christmas bird counts with his father. Ever since, any person who travels by foot or by canoe or in an automobile with my old man can't help observing whatever moves in the sky or flits across a soybean field or flutters through the pines. Why? Because in my dad's presence all that swoops, perches, or dives has a name, a profile, a history, a personality, a distinguished place on earth.

Last February my two brothers and I flew to Smithville for a family reunion. Pop's wife, Jackie, was on an archeological dig in Belize. Not for thirty-five years had we three sons been concurrently in the same room with our maker. We spent a memorable week together, taking walks and schmoozing, catching up on things.

The old guy moves a trifle slowly of late: the usual infirmities of age are exacting a toll. Still, he goes for a promenade daily over in Buescher State Park, with his dog, Scholar, by his side and my grandfather's old binoculars around his neck. Meticulously, he records the bird activity while driving to and fro. His hope is that the years of data he has kept and computerized will help protect migratory-bird habitat and breeding areas in the future.

My heart still leaps up when I start walking with the old man. The same goes for my brothers, Tim and Dave. At Buescher Lake he pointed out to us a solitary sandpiper, then turned the glasses on two red-shouldered hawks screeching and circling high above. A great blue heron flying by suddenly swerved, dived, and grabbed a tiny carp. There was a great egret across the water, looking stately in some reeds.

At another point in our visit he stopped the car abruptly to watch a pair of Mexican eagles (caracaras) trying to wrestle a dead slider turtle across a field. Later he mentioned how eagerly he was anticipating the April return of chimney swifts migrating north from South America. For years he has counted the number of them that dive into the post office chimney near his house, in Smithville. On certain nights there are more than a thousand.

From his freezer Dad took a yellow-shafted flicker that he'd picked up off the road. He posed for pictures with the handsome bird, and we boys did also, proud to display our affection for the natural world: like father, like sons. All of us were touched by the mystifying architecture of feather, beak, and claw, the impressive palette of color, the beauty of living things that fly.

Whenever I walk outdoors with the old man, my eye is on the planet. We observe chipping sparrows, cliff swallows, the weather, foliage, beetles, crossbills. At age fifty-seven I am always asking him questions, same as when I was ten: "What kind of moth is that?" "Where do cattle egrets roost at night?" "Is there really such a thing as a black-bellied tree duck?" I am eager to share with him by picking out, with my sharp eyes, a bluebird feather or a tiny warbler. It's my way of saying thanks, I guess, and also "I love you."

Yesterday I took a break from work and sat on my kitchen stoop, eating a grapefruit, while starlings moved in and out of the nesting box, feeding their young. An almost-grown fledgling poked its head clear when the parents were gone, waiting for more food. My cats, Cookie and Carlos, sat underneath the box, staring upward, plotting murder and mayhem.

The starling is a common bird, but I am fascinated by its rites of passage, which have entertained me all my life. That nesting box is a gift that keeps on giving. Each spring it reaffirms the curiosity and sense of wonder (and commitment) passed on to me by my father. Every time the birds arrive, I bless Pop for his life.

•

John Nichols is the author of the New Mexico Trilogy—*The Milagro Beanfield War*, *The Nirvana Blues*, and *The Magic Journey*— as well as *The Sterile Cuckoo* and *Dancing on the Stones*, among other fiction and nonfiction books.

Metropolitan Mallards

With little fanfare, the museum welcomes
distinguished guests

Marie Winn

The Metropolitan mallards made their first appearance
on July 9, 1990. That was when Mary Doherty, who
supervises photographs and color transparencies of art-
works for the Metropolitan Museum of Art, looked up
from her desk in the museum's Jane Watson Irwin Library
and saw a mottled brown duck with three downy yellow
chicks marching across the brick-paved interior courtyard
outside her window. She nearly fainted, she recalls.

The mallards had chosen an unlikely nursery. Known
by the staff as the Scholars' Courtyard, it is a rectangular
area about eighty feet long and twenty feet wide. It has a
border of thick English ivy and a median strip containing
four small locust trees in ivy covered planters. Nobody sits
in this courtyard—there are no chairs or benches. It is
merely an elegant spot to look out upon. Indeed, nobody
can even get into the Scholars' Courtyard except through

a single door in the Irwin Library. Otherwise it is surrounded on all sides by museum buildings, two of them four stories high, the others six stories high.

From above, the courtyard is open to the elements— the sky, the sun, the rain, the snow. And of course it is also open to the birds of Central Park, on whose eastern edge the museum is located. It must have been from above that the mother mallard and her ducklings made their way in, for no nest was found on the ground.

Ms. Doherty speculated that the female had constructed her nest on an adjacent rooftop and then nudged the fluffy babies over the edge after they hatched. After all, as Hal Harrison observes in his *Field Guide to Eastern Birds' Nests*, "Perhaps more than any other waterfowl, mallards seek unnatural nesting sites." No nest was found on the rooftops, however, though a search was conducted.

How the Metropolitan mallards made their way into the courtyard will remain a mystery. Nevertheless Ms. Doherty accepted responsibility for them. First she called the nearby Central Park Children's Zoo for advice on suitable food. Corn-oats scratch for mom, special pellets for the kids, she was told. Next she consulted Vivienne Sokol, a licensed wildlife rehabilitator, who promised to help out when it came time to return the ducklings to the wild.

Then Ms. Doherty appealed for help to Albert Torres, a library technician at the adjoining Watson Library, whose windows also look out on the Scholars' Courtyard. Mr. Torres, whose job includes maintaining books and transporting them to and from the stacks, became deeply involved with the ducks.

"All the years I've been here we've never had ducks coming into the museum. It was exciting," he related. "After Mary indicated to me that there were some ducks in the courtyard I went to the main restaurant and asked them to give us some bread and lettuce. I moistened the bread to make it spongy so they could nip on it, and that's how the ducks survived until Mary got them the real duck food.

"I also knew that ducks need water," Mr. Torres continued. "At first I filled up a cafeteria tray for them. Then I suggested to the public relations people that we should get a kiddie pool—it was kind of a joke. But they went and got it, a light blue one with duck decorations inside. But we could see the babies had trouble climbing into it. So we called the carpenter shop and asked them to make a ramp for the ducklings, which they did. We had to wait patiently because the babies wouldn't go up the ramp without the mother going first. Once she checked it out, that's when they followed her."

His boss at the Watson Library, Patrick Conan, was equally enthusiastic about the ducks. "It gave us a good feeling to see the way they all marched behind the mother. When Mama moved, they moved. I think there's something we can learn from that. This duck family was proof positive that it all starts at home."

After the first few days of settling in, the mother duck began to fly out on her own. Though the courtyard is entirely enclosed by tall buildings, she had no trouble leaving, for unlike diving ducks such as scoters and mergansers, who need a broad expanse of water for a running start, mallards and other dabbling ducks can rise straight up into the air.

In mid-August the ducklings, now almost full-grown, began flapping their wings in preparation for flight. That's when Ms. Doherty started to worry. "We were afraid the babies couldn't get out of here without hurting themselves," she recalled. "It was a very fragile situation. We knew it was time to transfer them to a larger body of water, but we had to do it when the mother was gone— she was always very nervous and protective around the ducklings." It was time to call in the wildlife rehabilitator. "When Miss Sokol arrived on August 26," Ms. Doherty related, "the mother duck had just flown out on one of her trips. So we looked at each other and decided: 'Let's do it!'

"Miss Sokol had brought a big blue cloth and she dropped it over the babies as they huddled in the corner. We put them in a cardboard carton, drove them to the park, and released them in the north end of the rowboat lake. That was it.

"Albert saved the kiddie pool and ramp, and even the cardboard carton. He was convinced that the ducks were coming back. I spent the entire winter explaining to him that this wasn't going to happen."

On June 3 of the following year, Mary Doherty looked out into the Scholars' Courtyard and saw a mother duck with four ducklings marching behind her. "I couldn't believe it," she said. "I was in a complete state of shock."

And so it happened that Ms. Doherty became the primary food provider for the Metropolitan mallards the second year in a row. Once again she found herself purchasing large quantities of scratch and pellets at a feed store in Peekskill. Every morning, as before, she chopped up spinach, kale, watercress, and different kinds of lettuce for the ducklings' delectation. Once again Mr. Torres cleaned the pool and supervised the ducklings' welfare. And once again the duck family thrived, though their caretakers came to believe it was not the same female. "Last year's mom was very autocratic," Ms. Doherty explained. "The second one was much more laid back."

By mid-July the ducklings were flapping their wings. And although the museum sent out no press announcements heralding the second release of the Metropolitan mallards, I managed to witness the event.

It happened on July 18. As chance would have it, I was watching birds that day in a secluded cove of the rowboat lake. I was just getting ready to leave when a green Parks Department van pulled up a few feet away from me and three people stepped out—Vivienne Sokol, Mary Doherty, and Albert Torres. Mr. Torres was looking dejected. Recalling the experience in tranquility a few weeks later he admitted: "I got too attached to the ducks. I'm not married. I have no kids, so now I know what it's like being a parent. You raise the kids and then you have to let them go."

After a quick inspection of the site Miss Sokol (as she prefers to be addressed) announced that this was a good place to do it. Thereupon Mr. Torres returned to the van and brought out a large cardboard carton. Written on its side were the words Save for Ducks.

He carried the carton to the water's edge and gently tipped it over so that one of the flaps formed a little ramp into the water. Then he began to make low, soothing sounds to encourage the ducks to emerge: "Quack. Quack-quack."

"There goes one. And two!" Ms. Doherty called out with excitement. Two ducklings scooted out and sailed into a nearby clump of reeds. A pause.

"Come on you guys!" Mr. Torres exhorted and resumed his quacking. Miss Sokol gave the carton a sharp rap and a third duckling was soon paddling rapidly in the direction of his two siblings.

The last bird remained in the back left corner of the carton and no amount of quacking could persuade it to leave. Drastic measures were needed, and Mr. Torres and Miss Sokol obliged. They lifted the carton and tipped it upside down. The fourth duckling was out.

"Don't go there! You're going the wrong way!" Mr. Torres shouted as the duckling headed towards the open part of the lake, where danger lurked in the form of row-boaters, gulls, and rapacious black-crowned night-herons. As if understanding Mr. Torres' cries, the young mallard reversed its direction. Everyone sighed with relief as Number Four disappeared in the reeds.

"We've done it again," said Ms. Doherty, and she, Mr. Torres, and Miss Sokol shook hands happily. Snapshots were taken and everyone went home.

Two weeks later I revisited the lakeside release site. There a stocky man with a shock of snowy-white hair was feeding a noisy gathering of ducks.

"You haven't seen a little group of four ducks lately?" I asked.

"Oh yes," he answered matter-of-factly, "There they are."

Now I saw that there were really two distinct groups of mallards in the water, twelve in one and four in the other.

"I've known this bunch of twelve since they were tiny ducklings," he continued. "There's the mom, the one with the black bill. I call her Missy. But look. Those four over there are a slightly different color. They're obviously from a different brood. They showed up here about two weeks ago. I don't know where they came from."

•

Marie Winn also contributed "Brooklyn's Rare Bird" to this collection.

Canal Walk

When the barges disappeared,
the birds returned

Mark S. Garland

It was a chilly, gray day in early April and one of those years when winter didn't want to go away. I hadn't been out much, so I made the short trip to Georgetown, that upscale corner of Washington, D.C., known for its shops, galleries, bars, and restaurants. But I wasn't looking for any of this. I needed a dose of nature, a bit of birding. I parked south of M Street, walked through the Washington Harbor development and down to the banks of the Potomac River. A few steps to the left and I had reached the mouth of Rock Creek. A group of Wood Ducks was quietly paddling in the river, dipping now and then for morsels of food brought down by the creek. The thin fog switched to drizzle and then back to fog. I stood alone, gazing across the river to the bare trees of Theodore Roosevelt Island. Soon this natural memorial to the great champion of conservation would be green again. Looking out over the river, it was easy to forget the urban scene at my back.

I turned around and strolled next to the creek, the towers of the Watergate to my right. At the first junction I turned left onto a well-worn footpath that paralleled the still waters of a broad ditch. I was stepping onto the towpath of the Chesapeake and Ohio Canal and into a national historical park named for the old waterway. Just a few miles from here, on July 4, 1828, President John Quincy Adams hoisted the first shovel-full of dirt to begin an ambitious engineering project. The goal was to create a water connection between the Potomac and Ohio rivers. The goal was never met, but 185 miles of canal were built from Georgetown upriver to the small industrial city of Cumberland in western Maryland.

I decided to walk along the canal for a while, following a path of dirt packed by the hooves of thousands of barge-pulling mules. Red brick city buildings flanked the path for half a mile or so. A Northern Mockingbird sang a few phrases from its perch high in a flowering silver maple, and then scolded me with three harsh notes before dropping into a small thicket across the canal. Mallards paddled quietly just below a wooden barge, which sat on blocks waiting for the weather to warm. In a few weeks, park rangers dressed in nineteenth-century costumes would teach history by taking school classes and families on barge rides through the locks.

I kept walking. In fifteen minutes the buildings gave way to forest. Big sycamore trees, easy to recognize by their mottled white trunks, towered above an understory of shoulder-high shrubs whose leafless branches were adorned with little yellow flowers. I reached for one of the twigs, gave it a little scratch, and inhaled. Spicebush is well-named, and it's almost an involuntary instinct for me to release a bit of its fragrance.

My olfactory reverie was interrupted suddenly. A loud series of raps on wood told me a Pileated Woodpecker was nearby. It took a bit of searching, but I finally found the crow-size bird on a thick, high branch of a sycamore. I looked to see if it had a red mustache stripe; it did, so it was a male. I listened more carefully to the sounds coming from the woods that separated the canal from the river. There were sharp chips emanating from brushy areas. I mentally ticked off Northern Cardinal and White-throated Sparrow. Then I heard a similar but louder and more metallic single note. Hairy Woodpecker, I thought, with satisfaction. Maybe I could find six species of woodpeckers today.

The C&O Canal is lined by mature forest for almost its entire length, making it an outstanding habitat for woodpeckers. That wasn't true during the canal's nine-teenth-century heyday. Old photos show that a few big shade trees were left near the lock-keepers' houses, but otherwise the riverside forest had been removed. In 1924, when the canal was failing as an economic venture, defeat-ed soundly by the railroads, a damaging flood resulted in the abandonment of the waterway. In the fertile soils of the Potomac floodplain, trees came back quickly. A forest was reborn, and some of the trees got big in a hurry.

In the late 1940s, after World War II, there was a surge of interest in nature and birding around Washington. The Audubon Society of the District of Columbia (now the Audubon Naturalist Society) became very active. The vig-orous forests and small wetlands lining the old C&O Canal became a favorite field-trip destination.

This was also an era of rapidly growing suburbs, and a time when ambitious highway projects were in vogue. The old canal lands seemed like an ideal site for a new river-side highway. In 1950, Congress was presented with a pro-posal to build such a highway. The idea was debated for several years. In early 1954, the *Washington Post* published an editorial urging that the road be built. Supreme Court Associate Justice William O. Douglas, an ardent outdoors-man, disagreed. He wrote a letter to the newspaper chal-lenging its editors to join him for a walk along the entire canal. Once they saw it, he argued, they would want to protect it.

The editors printed his letter and accepted the challenge. In late March 1954, the hike was made. Douglas and eight others, including *Post* editors and conservation activists, walked the entire distance; many others hiked with the group partway, and thousands came out to see the walkers and cheer them on. The *Post* changed its position, and the ensuing momentum for protection led to the designation of the C&O Canal as a national monument in 1961, upgraded to a national historical park in 1971.

I heard a loud, staccato rattling across the canal. Sure enough, it was another Pileated Woodpecker, this time a female. I wondered if Douglas and his crew might have heard Pileated Woodpeckers here as they neared the end of their famous trek. Maybe not; the trees would have been smaller then, and Pileateds need big, old trees. The male flew over to the same tree as the female, landing a few feet above her. He called, and then she called again. I kept walking.

I also kept finding birds. My woodpecker list grew to five as I saw two Downy Woodpeckers, two Red-bellied Woodpeckers, and a Northern Flicker. A Rusty Blackbird sipped from a puddle in the path. A flock of Cedar

Waxwings sat high in a slippery elm. An Eastern Towhee dug noisily through the leaf litter beneath some dense shrubs; it took a few minutes to get a look at him. He'd given away his identity earlier with his characteristic upslurred *thweep*, but I wanted to see him. I thought about the first towhee I'd ever seen, during a hike up in the Blue Ridge Mountains with my high-school buddies Mike Rosen and Steve Butler. We saw lots of towhees on that hike but didn't identify them until we reached a little store at hike's end and leafed through the pages of a field guide on the shelf. That was the first bird I ever looked up in a book.

Mike, Steve, and I had become friends a few years earlier, during junior high. At age fourteen we undertook the first big adventure of our lives. Over one summer week, the three of us bicycled the entire length of the C&O Canal. We did part of it twice; none of our parents wanted to drive us all the way to Cumberland. They took us to Hancock instead, so we cycled sixty miles west and then all the way back from Cumberland to Georgetown. We camped each night at one of the many simple "Hiker Biker Overnighter" campsites that had been established by the National Park Service. We stopped at riverside towns two or three times to buy groceries. I had trouble the first day and called home for help. Mom and Dad drove up, helped me fix the jury-rigged gear rack on my bike, and took two-thirds of my stuff back home. After that, the journey was great fun.

We rode thirty to forty miles every day. My old bike had just one speed, but that was okay, since the canal had no hills. We enjoyed the beautiful forests and sweeping river views. We saw lots of animals. Traveling quickly and quietly by bike, we managed to sneak up on critters that were lounging on the path. We saw countless woodchucks and cottontail rabbits this way, and also glimpsed a few red foxes. All would dash away in a frenzy once they spotted us. Much of the old canal bed was dry, but wherever there was water there were turtles—hundreds and hundreds of turtles. Nights were enlivened by the sounds of crickets, katydids, and owls. It seemed like a great wilderness adventure to us, three suburban kids from the television generation. I'm amazed our parents let us do it. Justice Douglas had argued that the canal's greatest value was its wilderness character. That character remains.

I only wish I'd been aware of birds back then. Birds came later, starting with that towhee in the mountains. I continued to walk upriver along the canal, crossing underneath the Francis Scott Key Bridge, still watching and listening for birds. I heard Golden-crowned Kinglets, then heard and saw a Brown Creeper, looking like a tree-climbing mouse with wings. I walked beneath a noisy flock of Common Grackles, heard a Song Sparrow sing, and spotted a Yellow-bellied Sapsucker, my sixth species of woodpecker for the day. Only one other species occurs around Washington, the Red-headed Woodpecker, but I knew not to expect that species inside the city. With birds, anything is possible, but I'd have to go twenty miles upriver to have a reasonable chance of finding this scarce bird.

I followed a little side path down to the river's edge. The fog had lifted just a bit, leaving a low overcast. An invisible roar came from above every few minutes as jets took off from nearby Reagan National Airport. They flew above the clouds; there were birds in the air beneath them. I saw Ring-billed Gulls and a few Herring Gulls. Six crows flew over from Virginia, one giving the nasal call of a Fish Crow. Tree Swallows swept back and forth, dropping close to the river's surface from time to time. I looked just above the water surface and saw a few flying insects, perhaps mayflies. Tree Swallow food.

Just as I started walking back to the towpath, a pair of buzzy notes made me stop. Eastern Phoebe, I thought—my first for the year. It's about time, I chided myself: phoebes come back in March. I hadn't been getting out enough. The phoebe called again, this time giving three calls in rapid succession. I looked at the maple branches leaning out over the river, and there it sat, just about five feet above the river's edge. It might have been feeding on mayflies, too.

I wanted to make time jump forward a few weeks. The big push of migrant songbirds begins around April 25 and continues through much of May. These are the glory days for birding along the C&O. If it were early May, I'd be hearing Yellow-throated Warblers singing from the sycamores and Baltimore Orioles from the elms. There would be Northern Parulas and Yellow-throated Vireos near the treetops, Yellow-billed Cuckoos and Black-throated Green Warblers at mid-canopy, Wood Thrushes and Black-throated Blue Warblers a bit lower in the trees.

I could head out to Carderock, where migrating Scarlet Tanagers always congregate in early May, or to Great Falls, where Prothonotary Warblers nest. I could visit Violette's Lock to see Orchard Orioles and Warbling Vireos, or Sycamore Landing, where transient thrushes and American Redstarts often concentrate, and where Cerulean Warblers nest in the treetops. Sycamore Landing is the most distant of these locations, but it's still only about twenty miles from Washington. I could go to Pennyfield Lock, where as a beginner I added many warblers to my life list . . .

But it wasn't early May, it was early April. I turned around and headed back toward Georgetown. I intercepted a mixed-species feeding flock and picked out Carolina Chickadee, Tufted Titmouse, Downy Woodpecker, and Yellow-rumped Warbler. I started to walk again, but the sound of a loud, harsh *chip* from across the canal stopped me in my tracks. I thought I recognized the sound, so I scanned along the canal's muddy bank. Sure enough, I spotted a small brown bird with a bold white eyebrow and a speckled breast standing on the mud with its tail end pumping up and down rhythmically. My first Louisiana Waterthrush of the year! I reconsidered my wish. May brings an exciting explosion of songbirds, but April brings so many of the year's first sightings. I felt energized, and my step became just a bit livelier.

Before long I was back in Georgetown. The light was starting to fade as evening approached, and I was getting pretty hungry. I thought about heading straight home, but instead I walked back to the end of the canal, then down the short path next to Rock Creek to the Potomac River shoreline. Wood Ducks were still there, swimming next to the foundation that once supported the canal's river lock, a structure long gone. A dozen Bonaparte's Gulls flew quickly downriver out by Roosevelt Island. I scanned the river edges and found three Great Blue Herons. A few moments later I saw a big bird fly out from behind the trees. It made a loud, harsh sound as it glided down to the water's edge: Black-crowned Night-Heron. Soon there was a second, then a third, finally half a dozen. They've probably come down from the zoo, I thought, where they nest in a colony above the Bald Eagle aviary.

Light was fading, and the night-herons and Wood Ducks had become silhouettes. I wanted to hear a Barred Owl call from Roosevelt Island, but I also wanted to get dinner. I waited for a few minutes, wondering how many times I had visited the C&O Canal, what percentage of my life had been spent on its towpath and adjoining trails. I did some quick figuring and realized that the number of visits was probably well over a thousand. I wished I could say thanks to Justice Douglas.

The Barred Owls never called, and so I headed home. I was pleased with all that I had seen and not worried about the birds I'd missed. I knew I'd be back many, many times.

•

Mark S. Garland is a senior naturalist at the New Jersey Audubon Society's Cape May Bird Observatory, the author of *Watching Nature*, and a nature commentator for "Metro Connection," a public radio program in Washington, D.C. He now lives in West Cape May.

Starling

For better or worse,
one city birder changed the nation

Kim Todd

I imagine him a quiet man, an unassuming man. While his relatives were making headlines all through the 1800s—stewing in jail on charges of bigamy, leading expeditions to the West, amassing large fortunes in business and giving interviews in *The New York Times* about the servant problem—Eugene Schieffelin was working for the family drug manufacturing company, attending meetings of the New York Zoological Society, and reading Shakespeare.

But he would have a more lasting effect on this country than any of his sisters, brothers, or nephews. They may have improved a neighborhood, or fashioned a law, but Eugene changed the American landscape from coast to coast.

What was he thinking that day as he went to Central Park with eighty newly imported starlings in cages? He must have pulled his wool coat tighter around him to protect against the cold, and wrapped his scarf around his face an extra time. It was March 6, 1890, and the temperature averaged twenty-three degrees. Snow had fallen all morning, occasionally turning to sleet, and then easing back to fluffy white flakes. It made icy statues of trees and bushes in the park, softening the accusing fingers of bare twigs into gestures of pale grace. Upstate, currant and strawberry farmers worried for their crops in the unseasonable weather; in the city, families hitched their horses to sleighs and prepared to go joyriding through the streets of New York.

It was a heady era, full of electricity and excitement. Sideshows and fortune tellers lured crowds to Coney Island. Chicago scrambled to raise money to hold the World's Fair, and New York hoped it would fail. One businessman was arrested when his product "hop soda" turned out to be beer. One businesswoman launched an international matchmaking service to link American desire for noble titles to the European desire for American money.

As the world was growing faster and dirtier, hurtling with increasing speed toward a goal that was never quite clear, people wondered if art could save them. Poets were so revered that John Whittier instructed his barber to burn all his hair clippings to keep them from overeager fans. Robert Browning's death made front page headlines for nearly a week. There was a movement afoot to keep the Metropolitan Museum of Art open on Sundays to lure people out of the saloons. Schieffelin, in his own attempt to civilize the beast his country had become, wanted to introduce all the birds mentioned in the plays of Shakespeare, to offer scraps of poetry on the wing.

At sixty-four, he must have had to watch his footing. Underneath the layer of snow, the cobblestones of the streets were buried under four inches of mud, frozen now and slick. I imagine Eugene, carrying one cage in each hand, each bout of squawking threatening to knock him off balance. His servants followed with the rest. Finally, under a tree that looked like it might be hospitable when the ice melted off its branches and was replaced by leaves and buds, Eugene stopped and set the cages on the ground. He paused for a moment, breathing in the chill air. Then one by one, he opened the latches, and the birds stepped out onto the snow-covered grass.

Dazed from months of traveling, first on rocking ships, then in bumping carriages, the starlings lingered near the cages. Some flexed their wings, still in winter plumage, flashing hundreds of white spots on black feathers. But they didn't go anywhere, just wandered a few feet in one direction, then another. At four-thirty, the clouds pulled away, leaving a clear sky darkening into the deep blue of evening. Shouts and laughter filled the streets as the sleighs flew by, some carrying a couple, flushed and romantic, others whisking a whole gleeful family. Hats and mittens littered the sidewalk. Eugene, growing cold and thinking about dinner, finally rushed at his birds, waving his arms and half yelling, half cheering them on, "Go, go, go." And first one, and then the whole group, took off, circling higher and higher into the black sky on blacker wings.

At two A.M., just as the last sleigh bells were falling silent, a pair of starlings found their way to the roof of the Museum of Natural History and ducked out of the cold. They fluffed their feathers, preened briefly, and settled in for the night. Soon, if the hole was large enough, protected enough, they would begin to build a nest. It was almost spring, after all.

Schieffelin, back in his Madison Avenue home, was in bed. His wet coat and shoes crackled and hissed and sent up plumes of steam as they dried by the fire. The empty cages were stacked nearby, a few feathers still tangled in the wire mesh. Lost in a deep sleep, with the blanket pulled up to his chin, the drug manufacturer snored and mumbled and dreamt of waking to a world echoing with the same bird song that Shakespeare heard.

Conservation biologists now view Schieffelin as an eccentric at best, a lunatic at worst. But he was not alone in his affection for the birds of the poets or his desire to see them in the New World. Throughout the United States "acclimatization" societies were releasing birds they thought would benefit or improve the landscape. Other bird lovers before Schieffelin freed starlings—in New Jersey in 1844 and in Oregon in 1889—but those birds did not thrive. House sparrows were introduced at least twenty times between 1850 and 1900, including a release of a thousand in Philadelphia by city officials. In 1881, the popular turn-of-the-century naturalist John Burroughs received a shipment of skylarks from a friend in England and wrote back, "Only seven out of the 24 sent reached me, and two of those died on my hands. The rest I let out on a field back of the hill, and two of them, at least, are still there, and, I think, will breed. When you come over I think you can hear the original of Shelley's skylark."

In 1871, James Edmund Harting wrote *The Ornithology of Shakespeare*, which listed all the birds that appeared in the plays and sonnets, as well as the quotations that named them. While sparrows, larks, and nightingales twitter their way through play after play, the only time the starling appears is in *Henry IV*, Part One.

In the crucial scene, King Henry demands that Hotspur, a passionate and willful soldier, release his prisoners, but Hotspur refuses. The enemy has captured Hotspur's brother-in-law, Mortimer, and Hotspur is withholding his prisoners until the king agrees to pay the ransom. The king loses his temper, declares Mortimer a traitor, and instructs Hotspur never to speak of his captured brother-in-law again. After the king leaves, Hotspur fumes:

> He said he would not ransom Mortimer,
> Forbade my tongue to speak of Mortimer,
> But I will find him when he is asleep,
> And in his ear I'll hollow "Mortimer!"
> Nay,
> I'll have a starling shall be taught to speak
> Nothing but "Mortimer," and give it him
> To keep his anger still in motion.

Maybe Schieffelin should have read his beloved bard more closely. In Shakespeare's imagination, the starling was not a gift to inspire romance or lyric poetry. It was a bird to prod anger, to pick at a scab, to serve as a reminder of trouble. It was a curse.

Helium balloons, Roman candles, rockets, whirling shiny objects, noisemakers shot from flare pistols, fire-crackers blasted from twelve-gauge shotguns, explosions of propane gas, artificial owls, airplanes, distress calls broadcast on mobile sound equipment, chemicals derived from peppers, chemicals that cause erratic behavior, chemicals that cause kidney failure, chemicals that make birds freeze to death.

These are the ways farmers have sought to protect their crops from starlings. None has had lasting success.

The medium-sized black bird, with a glossy purple and green sheen and a talent for mimicry, can be a charmer when first introduced. Wolfgang Amadeus Mozart kept a pet starling, which he found in a shop whistling the theme from one of his concertos. He kept it for several years, and penned a poem in its honor when it died. Pliny wrote with admiration of a starling which could recite phrases in both Greek and Latin, and Samuel Pepys noted in his diary that he witnessed "a starling which do whistle and talk the most and best that I have ever seen anything in my life." The very name "starling" calls to mind a creature of the night sky, of the heavens, almost divine. But as their numbers increased, along with awareness of the dangers of introducing exotic species, starlings' popularity took a nose dive.

When Schieffelin died in 1906, the birds were nesting outside the Museum of Natural History, in a church on 122nd Street and Lennox Avenue, and in the Boys' High School building in Brooklyn, but they hadn't yet reached Kansas, California, or Alaska. From the eighty he released in 1890, and the forty more he set free in April of 1891, the number of starlings in North America has grown to 200 million. They decimate fruit crops and out compete other cavity nesters, including eastern bluebirds, flickers, great crested flycatchers, and red–bellied woodpeckers. A single flock of starlings, called a "murmuration," can reach up to a million or more birds, blanketing the sky with feathers and the ground with excrement. They thrive in cities, along highways, at garbage dumps. Early last year, an Ohio town hired an extermination company to poison the birds that were roosting nearby and rendering the sidewalks slick with droppings.

If starlings have a noteworthy genetically programmed personality trait, it is aggression. They wait until other birds create nesting holes, then harass the architects until they abandon the site. Sometimes the starling enters a cavity while the original owner is gone. When the bird returns, the starling leaps onto its back, clinging and pecking all the way to the ground. Even when it has claimed a nesting cavity, a starling may continue to abuse other birds breeding nearby, plucking their eggs out of the nest and dropping them on the ground.

Bird lovers watch in dismay as the native species they cherish are chased off by the dark intruders. One ornithologist observed a starling dangle a piece of food in front of the nesting cavity of a downy woodpecker. When the woodpecker chick reached out of the hole for the bait, the starling dispatched the youngster with one quick jab of the beak. Another bird lover watched from his kitchen window one year in late winter as a pair of starlings moved into two cottonwood trees that had formerly hosted only native birds. Within days, another dozen pairs joined the original duo. As he watched through his binoculars over the course of the next few months, the starlings scared off American kestrels, northern flickers, olive-sided flycatchers, tree swallows, and many other species. By June, the trees offered refuge to twenty-seven starlings, and nothing else.

At the point in history when Schieffelin hatched his plot, America's relationship with England was rife with ambiguity. America, like a younger sister, admired her older sibling's poise and experience, but chafed at her patronizing tone. Thoreau and Whitman valorized the species of plants and animals in the United States as more wild and hearty than their tame English counterparts, but American thoughts still dwelt on the glories of Britain. As such a young nation, with many people so new to the land, America had a shortage of stories that took place on its own soil. Without a literary tradition, the Americans didn't know what could happen in their landscape. Was there romance in America, or did lovers need to waken to the song of the lark to experience the joys of Romeo and Juliet? Could Hamlet have seen providence in the fall of a bluebird, or did it have to be a sparrow? The desire to see ourselves as heroes and heroines of stories that we know and love easily translates to a desire for the literal artifacts of those tales. The architects of Yale University paint the stone walls with acid to give them the aged look of Cambridge. A traveler clips a sprig of heather from the moors where Heathcliff may have roamed and plants it in her garden in Arizona. Children at Disneyland hop on Mr. Toad's Wild Ride and watch the landscape of *Wind in the Willows* careen past.

The New York drug manufacturer's error was on such a grand scale because he underestimated the dark potential of both language and biology. Wanting to release all of Shakespeare's birds indiscriminately, because they were part of the landscape, because they were in poetry, he viewed them as pleasant, or, more importantly, benign. Birds and poetry were pretty. They uplifted the spirit. They kept people out of saloons. Nature and art, particularly when they are beautiful, are often viewed as good, which is an underestimation of both. Left unrealized are the dangers of dreaminess, of looking at bright colors of plumage or blur of flight, rather than the ruthless engine of DNA.

Though not in the way he intended, Eugene Schieffelin successfully incorporated the birds of Shakespeare into the tale of his country, just as surely as Shakespeare wrote the birds into the history of England when he penned *Henry IV*. Not much is known about why Schieffelin did what he did. No journal entries. No direct quotes. Just a few facts told and retold in scientific journals, in birding guides, and in biology textbooks with the same smug sense of horror. In the century since they first flew free in Central Park, starlings have started to mimic the noises of American urban life, gathering the threads of a narrative. The rumble of cars and hum of machinery may work its way into the clicks and whistles that make up their repertoire. They have been reported to imitate dogs barking, doors slamming, hammers hitting wood. And as they pick up the cadences of jack-hammers and squealing brakes, the starlings in Florida, Ohio, and New Mexico add their voices to the story of America—a story, like Schieffelin's, of dreaminess, disaster, and possibilities beyond the imagination.

•

Kim Todd is the author of *Tinkering with Eden,* a *Library Journal* selection as one of the Best Sci-Tech Books of 2001. She lives in Missoula, Montana.

JJA in New Orleans

Following in Audubon's footsteps
offers dubious rewards

Mary Durant and Michael Harwood

New Orleans was a city John James Audubon knew
well. But he disliked cities, and this place was no
exception: "New Orleans, to a man who does not trade in
dollars or any other such stuff," he once declared, "is a mis-
erable spot." He came here to live for brief periods only to
scratch for said dollars and to paint new birds and to gain
a reputation. He was nearly penniless when he arrived in
the winter of 1820–21. He remarked that in earlier years
(when he had come here on business) he could at least
afford to go to the theater. Now he couldn't even spend a
dollar to attend the "Quartroon Ball"—a high point of the
local social season, a coming-out party for the mulatto
mistresses-to-be of New Orleans' white gentlemen. He
stood outside for a while to listen.

Still, New Orleans could entertain even the thread-
bare stranger. JJA wrote about a Sunday when "The Levee

early was Crowded by people of all Sorts as well as Colors, the Market very aboundant the Church Bell ringing the Billiard Balls Knocking, the Guns heard all around. What a display this for a Steady Quaker of Philada or Cincinnati." The room that he and Joseph Mason rented for ten dollars a month, on Barracks Street near the corner of Royal in the oldest part of the city, was "between Two Shops of Grocers and divided from them and our Yellow Landlady be Mere Board Partitions, receiving at once all the new Matter that issues from the thundering Mouths of all these groupes."

They lived near the French Market—"the Dirtiest place in all the Cities of the United States," said JJA—which was kept regularly supplied with freshly shot birds. Sometimes he could find a good specimen there to draw, although most of the birds hung for sale were either too damaged by shot to be useful to him or had been partly plucked. Even when he came across something in good condition the experience could be frustrating. He found "Grey Snipes" (probably willets, a species he had only just met) but "the Stupid Ass who sold me one Knew Nothing, Not even where *he* had Killed them." Naturally, he would rather have done all his hunting himself, but he couldn't do that and still earn a living and make a name for himself where it counted—in the city—and perhaps

convince the federal government to hire him as a naturalist for an exploring-surveying expedition. So, besides
prowling in the French Market, he employed other men
to do his hunting for him, around the rivers and swamps
and beaches and bays of southern Louisiana.

Meanwhile, once he was established in New Orleans,
he didn't do badly as an itinerant maker of black-chalk
portraits or as a drawing teacher. In fact, his success—
though mild and short-lived—sometimes surprised him.
On one occasion, going to the studio of the painter John
Vanderlyn to get a letter of recommendation, he had to
show his work to prove he was worthy. This took place in
front of a second visitor, a stranger, and when Audubon
left, with letter in hand, he was feeling humiliated by what
he'd been through. But the other visitor followed him
from the studio and stopped him on the street to compli-
ment him on his drawings and ask the price of a portrait.
"I thought how Strange it was," wrote JJA, "that a poor
Devil Like me Could steal the Custom of the Great
Vanderlein—but fortune if not *blind* certainly Must have
his Lunatic Moments."

When he and Mason came back to New Orleans
from Oakley and St. Francisville, he rented a furnished
room on St. Anne Street, until he found a house on
Dauphine Street, anticipating the arrival of Lucy and the

children. They joined him a week before Christmas 1821, but the family was together only three months before JJA's prospects once again soured and he and Mason left for Natchez, seeking greener pastures.

So we are here to look for three houses in the *Vieux Carré*, or French Quarter, of New Orleans, and to browse around the city. Most of this metropolis—all but the *Vieux Carré*, really—ought by rights to be a full-time swamp, and the entire area frequently flooded. The French Quarter was built on the only natural high ground, and everything else is on drained wetland and fill. A lot of it is six feet below sea level. More than twenty huge pumps and two hundred miles of drainage canals are needed to keep the city dry in normal circumstances, never mind floods or hurricanes. And if it weren't for levees along the Mississippi at the south and flood-diversion canals and seawalls on Lake Pontchartrain to the north, the city would often be drowned: one can look down into the streets from ships passing on the river at flood, and hurricanes sweep high tides from the Gulf across thirty miles of marsh, into the houses of the suburbs. Altogether an interesting prospect to live with. It must be largely responsible for the no-tomorrow character and spirit of the city. The bayous through the vast surrounding marshes are lined with trash.

Canals and ponds and bayous and marshes have been used as dumps; egrets and herons stalk among the drifts of garbage, just passing through, like the humans here. At the heart of the city (the *Vieux Carré*, the city that Audubon knew, beautiful old French and Spanish brick townhouses cramped gently together, narrow streets and delicate iron grillwork and green-glowing inner courtyards) there's a carny spirit, a sinister, whores-and-trash-on-the-midway carny spirit, people putting on the dog and the tourists and each other.

To live in the French Quarter means tourists, tourists, tourists. It's geared for tourists, caters to every taste. The Voodoo Museum, the old Absinthe House, St. Louis Cathedral, ice cream parlors, Antoine's, steaming nightlife, Topless Everything, porn shows, cheap souvenir shops, million-dollar antique shops, the state museum in the Cabildo, where the Spanish government was once housed and where JJA's *The Birds of America* is now displayed.

Doors and shutters are open to saloons and music, one set of shutters open to a pale figure in a bed in a tumbled darkened room. Other windows are shuttered tight and bolted against the light, eyes, prowlers. Crowds overflow from the sidewalks. Tourists, tourists, tourists. Beats and street people, the very young and the very old in rags and tatters. Drunks, dudes, pimps, peddlers, drug heads. A ravaged beauty (patrician features, real jewels on her fingers, scabby veined legs, sneakers cut down into slippers) who elbows angrily (snarling) through sightseers ganged up at the mouth of a saloon to hear Dixieland. In the street, boys dancing to the music for coins. Across the way, a balcony musician with lounging friends, a loop of Spanish moss hanging from the neck of his banjo. On the next corner, an old black man with a tambourine, his wife singing in a voice like Leadbelly's, the tambourine for rhythm and to catch the coins.

The French Market, where JJA browsed for unfamiliar birds, has been largely remodeled into cafes, boutiques, rest rooms. Tourists, tourists, tourists. Beyond, one small section is still a market. What fruits and vegetables there! Vine-ripened shining tomatoes, lacquer-green bell peppers, plump lavender garlic buds, striped green melons, flats of red strawberries . . .

No game is exposed for sale, though walking down the long, roofed aisle of the open-air market, sun-dazzle on the street to either side, food-dazzle in the middle, one can imagine the marsh-hares and raccoons and deer, the ducks and snipe and owls and robins, each split, gutted, tied up by a foot. That business ceased not so long ago. West of here in the Garden District, where the khaki-colored trolleys run along a grassy track, and houses of some years and dignity stand surrounded by gardens in the shade of old trees, a widow of an old New Orleans family, her parlor guarded by a Doberman, told us over cocktails that her mother had spoken of game for sale in the French Market and of men crying game through the streets of the Garden District, though of course anyone with money and leisure shot his own. Said our hostess, "I cannot think of a man of my father's generation who did not go hunting, and my father used to bring home hogsheads of ducks." But now game is rare in New Orleans. Just recently a friend had brought her a brace of snipe, she said. "It was like being given a string of diamonds."

One of Audubon's three New Orleans homes is gone. The other two, seen only from the outside, are as small and unprepossessing as one would expect for domiciles of an indigent artist. Neither is open to the public.

We went to Audubon Park—"New City Park" when it was created in 1871, but renamed in 1876 by the city council "in consideration of the distinguished ability of the late John James Audubon as an ornithologist and an artist, his many virtues as an exemplary gentleman and the high honor he reflects upon this his native state." It's four hundred acres fronting on the river in the southwest corner of the city: golf course, small zoo, aquarium (closed due to vandalism), open-air theater, swimming pool, tennis courts. The only sign of JJA about the park is a heroic bronze statue on a ten-foot granite pedestal—the artist in buckskin, shoulder-length hair, shot-pouch and powder-horn hanging at his side, tablet in one hand, brush in the other, head back, eyes on a presumed bird in one of the surrounding trees.

This figure came to stand in the park through the devotion of Mary Fluker Bradford, daughter of a St. Francisville pupil of Lucy Audubon. Mrs. Bradford wrote a brief, chatty biography of JJA in 1900, earned a thousand dollars for it, and donated the proceeds to start the Audubon Monument Fund. Ten years later, she had ten thousand dollars and commissioned one of the best sculptors of the day, Edward Virginius Valentine. The statue is now partly hemmed in by chain-link fence and barbed wire while close by are two of the planet's few score remnant whooping cranes, residents in the zoo.

•

Mary Durant and Michael Harwood are the coauthors of *On the Road with John James Audubon*, awarded the John Burroughs Medal for nature writing in 1981. Harwood is also the author of *The View from Hawk Mountain*. He died in 1990. Durant lives in California.

The Magic Hedge

Weary travelers find sanctuary
in a Chicago park

Julie Zickefoose

A weekend in May, and I find myself in Chicago. I'm a
bird painter, and a couple of my watercolors are
included in a group show celebrating the beauty of
American wood-warblers. I've left my eighty-acre Appa-
lachian sanctuary reluctantly, lured only by the prospect of
meeting other bird artists in this huge, clamorous city. It's
high migration time, and were I home, I'd be ambling
through the old orchard, sorting through the calls of mag-
nolia and prairie and blue-winged and chestnut-sided
warblers, drunk with delight as my binoculars find the
source of each song.

I can't help but wonder what I'm doing here when
the birds are pouring through the trees back in southern
Ohio. I wish I could say I have a love-hate relationship
with big cities, but that would be too charitable. Living as
I do, eighteen miles from the nearest town, back of

beyond, I've grown used to the music of crickets and birds, the slow track of clouds across the sky. A lungful of bus exhaust, the shriek of a siren, the jostle of a surging crowd—they all make me want to run like a whitetail the shortest way home.

Still on country time, I rise at dawn and begin to explore the city on foot and by bus. Might as well take in what I can before the show opens in the evening. But the town is closed up tight as a clam. Everyone must still be sleeping. I'm window-shopping a few blocks from the Lake Michigan shore, in an aimless sort of way, until the art and natural history museums open for the day. And I am flabbergasted to find real live warblers everywhere, sitting dazed on the sidewalks of these concrete canyons. Other people out on this quiet Sunday morning don't seem to notice this phenomenon; they step over the tiny birds as they would discarded candy wrappers. I suspect that city dwellers, having no idea that such beautiful creatures exist, fail to recognize them when they're right under their noses. I smile wryly at myself. You can take the girl out of the country ... I scurry about, trying to catch the weakened ones, or at least shoo them out of the major thoroughfares, all thoughts of the unaccustomed pleasures of museums, fancy coffee, and pastries banished by the birds' plight.

To understand why there are suddenly dozens of warblers huddling in sidewalk cracks and against the bases of lampposts, I think about the weather the night before, when these little birds fell out of the sky. It was damp, and foggy. The constellations, which help guide birds on their nocturnal migration, were obscured. To a warbler coming north across the dark plains, the great orange glow of Chicago must look like sunrise. Disoriented and weary, thousands circle brightly lit skyscrapers and communications towers. Many hit glass and guy wires; millions perish beneath such structures each spring and fall. My naturalist's eye picks out small carcasses along the sidewalk. The lucky ones are simply exhausted this quiet Sunday morning.

My footfalls echo eerily in this vast maze of hard, shiny surfaces. I can't imagine a warbler trying to regain the sky, flying straight up out of a solid block of tall buildings. There's not a tree anywhere in sight, nothing to hide in or cling to. On my odd little mission of mercy, I feel the city dwellers' curious eyes on me; they must think I'm addled. I feel as out-of-place as the warblers must. I see a tiny yellowthroat being blown about in the backdraft of a city bus and I sprint into the intersection to pick it up. He's exhausted but unhurt, his eyes bright and defiant in a black bandit mask. Smiling, I slip the little bird into a buttoned coat pocket, pull my city map out of another, consult it, and walk a few blocks to the nearest bus stop. I've got a plan.

Montrose Harbor Park is about five miles north of downtown Chicago, in an area called the Loop because of the pattern formed by the elevated train tracks nearby. The park occupies a curving coat-hook of land that juts due east out of the western shore of Lake Michigan then doubles back on itself. It contains Frisbee-friendly lawns, a golf course, a marina, and a beach. A bird flying along the heavily developed western shore of this great inland sea would notice the protected harbor that nestles behind the hooked peninsula, as well as the area's dense shrubbery and leaning willows that trail their branches in the water. For fully twenty miles of shoreline north of this park there is nothing but urban sprawl. And the concrete and glass continue to the south as far as the eye can see. For tired birds, Montrose Harbor Park is an oasis in a desert.

Just as the hook of land curves back toward the shore, at the southernmost elbow of the parkland, there is a row of bushes called the Magic Hedge. Birdwatchers have given it this name because any species is likely to turn up in it at any time, sometimes in spectacular numbers.

The hedge is nothing special botanically, mostly privet interspersed with native saplings. It's about fifteen feet wide and stretches about two hundred feet long, and it's surrounded by mown lawn. Very unprepossessing, but it's the last real cover migrant birds can use to feed and rest before they continue their great flight along urbanized Lake Michigan on the way north in the spring. In the fall, exhausted migrants plummet into the hedge after they've flown the length of the lake on their way south. The Magic Hedge doubtless saves many small lives. On September 23, 1990, the Chicago Audubon Society's bird-sighting hot line reported that more than five thousand birds were seen in the hedge, at rates of up to eight hundred songbirds an hour. I would hate to be a caterpillar in the Magic Hedge.

I disembark the bus and make my way to the lakefront and the hedge. I barely get my pocket open before the little yellowthroat slips out and dives into the greenery. He'll make it now. Glowing with satisfaction, I scan the privet bushes with my binoculars and see the first sedge wren of my life, as if in reward for the small mitzvah I've done. Then I see another, and a third. Wow. I've waited all my life to see a sedge wren and now here are three in the middle of greater Chicago, bustling about in search of scales and aphids.

Other birders stand quietly nearby, watching wave after wave of birds plunge into the hedge. Inclined to feel sorry for urban birdwatchers, who awaken not to whip-poor-wills but to sirens and grinding gears, I feel a twinge of envy at the ease with which these Chicagoans are able to pick treasures from this scruffy little copse.

The Magic Hedge quietly gives its gift to birds and birders alike, year in and year out. This simple planting, doubtless intended to be merely a windbreak for the gales that come in off the lake, has been exploited by hoards of migrant birds and birdwatchers. I'd like to raise my babies in a world where Magic Hedges, like golf courses and marinas, are created not by dumb luck but are planned, planted, and part of city budgets. I sometimes wish we could go back and build such green spaces into every urban landscape.

A common yellowthroat, weighing no more than the few pennies in my pocket, can make its way, sight unseen, from its Canadian birthplace to Central America. Migrant birds are thought to have a kind of inner compass that urges them to fly in a given direction for a given period of time. Called the "vector navigation" hypothesis, it helps explain how a naive yellowthroat fledgling can start out one fine August morning in Ontario, knowing nothing of inland seas, concrete chasms, or mountain ranges, and end up in Costa Rica by Thanksgiving.

The mite that blinked back at me from my cupped hands might have spent the winter on a Latin American citrus plantation. He made it as far north as Chicago, only to be tossed about in the wake of a bus like a bit of cellophane. That I was there to give him a second chance at completing his journey seemed right. Neither of us belonged here, really. We were both just looking toward home.

•

Julie Zickefoose writes about birding for *Bird Watcher's Digest*, where her bird paintings also often appear. She's the author of *Natural Gardening for Birds* and *Enjoying Bird Feeding More*.